LONDON
ON TWO WHEELS

25 HAND-PICKED RIDES TO MAKE THE MOST OF THE CITY

CONTENTS

GETTING STARTED

Using the bike hire scheme is simple and easy. There's
no need to book – simply hire a bike, ride it, then return
it to any docking station, ready for the next rider.

The hire bikes are available 24 hours a day, every single day
of the year. You can choose from more than 10,000 bikes
at over 700 docking stations. With docking stations every
300–500m (330–550 yards), you will never be far from a bike.

YOUR THREE-STEP GUIDE

❶ Hire

- Go to the nearest docking station terminal with your debit
  or credit card and touch the screen to begin.
- Select 'Hire a Cycle', follow the on-screen instructions and
  take the printed release code. Note that each code is valid
  for 10 minutes and only at that docking station.
- You can hire up to four bikes at the same time – but you'll
  need a separate release code for each bike.

❷ Ride

- Take a moment to read the tips for safer cycling at the terminal.
- Choose your bike and check the tyres, brakes and bell.
- Type your five-digit release code into the docking point's silent
  keypad and pull the bike out when the green light appears.
- Adjust the saddle height and go.
- Remember that the bikes have lights that come on
  automatically when you start pedalling.

❸ Return
- Push the bike firmly into any empty docking point.
- Wait for the green light, which will show the bike is securely docked (otherwise the charges for your journey will continue).
- If the docking station is full, select 'No docking point free' at the terminal and follow the on-screen directions to get an extra 15 minutes free.
- To find a nearby space if the docking station is full, select 'Status of nearest docking station' at the terminal.
- Remember, if you're not using the bike, dock it back!
- If the bike is unsafe to ride, press the 'fault' button on the docking point within ten seconds of docking it. You will need to wait five minutes before hiring another bike.

WHAT YOU PAY

COSTS		
It costs £2 to access the bikes for 24 hours and the first 30 minutes of each journey is free. Longer journeys cost £2 for each extra 30 minutes or less.		
HIRE	Bike access for 24 hours	£2
RIDE	First 30 minutes of each journey	Free
	Each extra 30 minutes or less	£2
RETURN	You must return a bike within 24 hours	
You could be charged up to £300 if you damage a bike or do not return it.		

All journeys under 30 minutes are free from extra ride charges.

- Your bike access period begins once payment is taken, not when you first use the bike.
- The scheme accepts all major credit and debit cards – it does not accept cash or Oyster cards.
- You must be 18 or over to hire a bike and 14 or over to ride one.

REGISTER FOR YOUR OWN KEY

If you are a regular user of the bikes, consider becoming a member:

- Get your own key for quicker bike access. (There's a one-off £3 fee per key.)
- Buy yearly bike access for only £90 – that's just 25p a day.

PAY AS YOU PEDAL MEMBERSHIP

For quicker bike access without the cost of yearly membership, why not become a 'pay as you pedal' member? Register for a key online and select 24-hour bike access, then simply pay £2 when you hire your first bike of the day and any extra charges for journeys over 30 minutes. No yearly fee – just slot your key into the keypad, and away you go!

Register at tfl.gov.uk/santandercycles

SANTANDER CYCLES APP

The official Santander Cycles app is the only app to send bike release codes straight to your smartphone. So you can skip past the docking station terminal and get on your bike quicker. Simply register with your bank card, and use the app to 'Hire now' from a nearby docking station. Follow the instructions to get your bike release code. Tap the code into the docking point, and you're good to go. Each bike release code is valid for 10 minutes at your chosen docking station. You can also:

- See up-to-the minute information about which docking stations have bikes and spaces available.
- Plan a journey with an easy-to-follow map.
- Receive notifications – for example, summarising the cost at the end of your hire.
- View your recent journeys and charges.

Please note that the app doesn't reserve bikes. If there are no bikes available at the docking station, don't worry. Use the app to find a nearby docking station with bikes, and get another bike release code to use there.

CYCLING SAFETY & ETIQUETTE

Seeing London on two wheels is one of the best ways of getting to know and experiencing the city. However, the roads of the capital are very busy and although safety measures are continually being improved and developed, there are ways of cycling that can reduce risk.

Follow these tips to help enjoy your ride in London:

DOS:

- **DO** beware of blind spots around large vehicles – it's often safer to hang back.

- **DO** watch out for other vehicles and pedestrians and show your intentions by always giving clear hand signals.

- **DO** make yourself seen by wearing bright clothing in the day and reflective clothing or accessories at night.

- **DO** consider wearing a helmet.

- **DO** wait in front of other vehicles at traffic lights by using the advanced stop line for cyclists, if there is one.

- **DO** use only signed cycle routes or roads in the Royal Parks, or you may be fined.

- **DO** stop at zebra crossings for pedestrians.

DO avoid and report potholes to the local council with the FillThatHole app.

DO use the gears to make cycling easier.

DON'TS:

DON'T ride through red traffic lights – you may be fined £50.

DON'T cycle on the pavement or the wrong way up one-way streets (unless clearly marked for cyclists).

DON'T get too close to parked cars – beware of car doors opening suddenly.

DON'T use a mobile phone or earphones while cycling – you need to rely on all your senses when riding.

DON'T ride a bike when under the influence of alcohol or drugs.

DON'T cycle in the gutter – if the road is narrow, it may be safer to ride towards the middle of the lane to prevent dangerous overtaking.

Find out more about cycle training at tfl.gov.uk/cycletraining

CYCLING FUN

We all know that cycling is one of the most efficient eco-friendly modes of transport; whether it's simply getting you from A to B or a journey through one of the lovely routes in this book, it can be more relaxing than running and quicker than walking – allowing you to see more sites in the same time!

Cycling also has the added benefit of being a very sociable activity. Everyone remembers the experience of learning to ride their first bike and the people who helped them along the way. From athletes taking part in the Tour de France, to families and groups of friends out for a weekend bike ride, cycling tends to be a team activity, allowing you to chat along the way – be it giving each other a little encouragement or sharing observations about your new surroundings.

Whether you're a visitor to the city or a London local, there's always something new to see in the capital. And the chances are that seeing the sights on bike will enhance your experience and help you to remember it more clearly – you won't simply recall that you once visited the Albert Memorial, you'll remember cycling past it through the stunning surroundings of Hyde Park (pages 30–35), maybe with a friend or two.

CYCLING FIT

Cycling is a great way of increasing your fitness while getting out-and-about with friends and family, exploring new places and having fun along the way.

Why is cycling so good for you? Cycling keeps your heart and lungs healthy and fit, and burns calories. It's low impact because the bike supports your body weight, meaning it is kinder on your bones and joints than other aerobic exercise, like running.

Cycling outdoors in the fresh air increases your concentration and boosts your energy levels for the rest of the day. And because cycling predominantly uses the muscles in your lower body, it is a sure-fire way to achieve beautifully toned thighs, calves and bottom! What's not to love?

Regular exercise significantly lowers the risk of Type II diabetes, all types of cancer, high blood pressure and obesity. NHS guidelines for physical activity recommend a combination of aerobic and muscle-strengthening activities. Guess what? Riding a bike ticks all of these boxes.

Head to your nearest docking station and start enjoying London on two wheels!

GETTING TECHNICAL

Mid- to long-distance cycling is a form of aerobic exercise that is low to moderate intensity, involving the repetitive movement of the major muscles in the legs.

It relies primarily on the use of oxygen to meet the body's energy requirements. The heart rate increases and breathing becomes faster as the heart, lungs and blood vessels work harder to transport oxygen and nutrients to the working muscles, and to expel carbon dioxide.

Cycling harder results in aerobic energy production gradually being supplemented by anaerobic metabolism. At this point, muscles start to produce lactic acid, which quickly builds up in the blood. This build-up causes an increasing burning sensation in the legs, which eventually forces the rider to lower the exercise intensity until the lactate has dispersed.

GETTING THE MOST OUT OF YOUR RIDE

Saddle up

Setting the saddle at the right height for you is essential for comfort and efficiency and to avoid injury. Too low and your leg muscles will not work through their entire range, leaving your knee too bent. Having the seat too high will overextend or lock your knee and make your foot lose contact with the pedal, potentially irritating your hips and ankles too. Either way, riding with the saddle at the wrong height for you will result in knee pain and a much more tiring ride, as your body has to work much harder to get the bike moving.

Before you undock, stand alongside the bike and adjust the saddle height so it is level with your hip joint. When you sit on the bike, your leg should be slightly bent at the knee at the bottom of the pedalling stroke.

Get in gear

Your bike has three gears. Gear 1 is the lowest and easiest gear to start cycling in because it provides the least resistance. It is also very helpful in making uphill climbs easier.

When your legs feel warmed up, you can increase the resistance by twisting the handle towards you to increase the gear. Gear 3 provides the most resistance and the hardest workout. You will need it on steep downhill stretches.

Keep pedalling as you change gear for a smoother ride.

Step on it

The most efficient way to cycle is with the ball of your foot on the pedal. With your foot in this position, you will be able to produce more power and control. It will also reduce strain on your joints.

Sit up

Good cycling posture simply means: No slumping! Sitting up is better for your back and for your stability on the bike – especially when reaching out to indicate – and it will also help with visibility of the traffic around you.

BURN CALORIES BURN

Thirty minutes of cycling can burn from around 100 calories up to a whopping 700 calories, depending on various factors, such as your weight and the speed at which you cycle. The faster you cycle, the more calories you will burn. Have a look at this chart:

CALORIES BURNED ON A 30 MINUTE CYCLE

INDIVIDUAL'S WEIGHT: **65 kg**
SPEED: less than 10mph, **130 cals**
       10–12mph, **195 cals**
       12–14mph, **260 cals**

INDIVIDUAL'S WEIGHT: **85kg**
SPEED: less than 10mph, **170 cals**
       10–12 mph, **255 cals**
       12–14 mph, **340 cals**

The average traffic speed around central London is 14.5km/h (9mph), so on most of the routes you'll be burning 130–170 calories – about a bag of crisps. But on some of the quieter routes, such as the one on pages 139–143, which takes in Richmond Park, you could easily find yourself pushing the bike close to its top speed of 19km/h (12 mph), so burning 195–255 calories. Not only that, but the harder you work, the more you rev up your metabolism to keep on burning calories at a higher rate for the rest of the day.

WORKING HARDER

Intervals are a great way to improve fitness, leg strength and endurance, as well as burning more fat, faster. After warming up for 5–10 minutes in a low gear, simply alternate a period of higher intensity cycling with a period of lower intensity recovery.

You could choose a landmark and try pedalling faster until you get there. Or cycle faster in a higher gear. Your legs will soon feel like they're on fire!

FUEL

Cycling outdoors is harder work than it might seem, so you need to make sure you refuel. It's a good idea to carry some water in your bag, and take regular sips to keep you alert. If you are riding one of the longer routes, such as on pages 45–49, make sure you pack a snack and stop for a rest while taking in your surroundings! If you don't want to interrupt your cycle with a quick pit stop, make sure you eat something within 30 minutes of finishing your ride.

STRETCH

After your ride it's a good idea to spend two minutes stretching. Why? To maintain a healthy functional range of movement in your joints as well as to reduce muscle soreness. The three key stretches for your legs are: quadriceps, hamstrings and calf. Stretch to the point of tension, not pain, and don't bounce! Keep breathing and hold the stretch for 10–15 seconds.

THE ROUTES

In the following pages, you will find a range of 25 fabulous routes that you can follow using the bike hire scheme in London. The routes are divided by area of London and will take you along the River Thames and through much-loved cultural highlights. You can also venture further afield and cycle outside the hire zone. Remember, once you begin these routes, you won't be able to abandon your bike.

THE WILD WEST END

Wonder at the magnificence of Wren's Baroque masterpiece and then take a tour of London's legal heartland, and on through the alleys of Seven Dials to the maze and vibrancy of Soho, before crossing to the boulevards of Mayfair and the serenity of Hyde Park.

DISTANCE 6km (3¾ miles)
PROFILE Some gentle climbing
PICK-UP DOCKING STATION Godliman Street, St Paul's
DROP-OFF DOCKING STATION Upper Grosvenor Street, Mayfair or Park Lane, Mayfair

- Ride north uphill towards St Paul's Cathedral.
- Turn left on St Paul's Churchyard, which becomes Ludgate Hill.
- At Farringdon Street go straight on into Fleet Street.
- Turn right carefully through the modal filter into Shoe Lane.
- Turn left into Little New Street, left again into Printer Street and right into East Harding Street. (A left though the arch into Gough Square takes you to Dr Johnson's House.)
- East Harding Street becomes Pemberton Row, then West Harding Street.
- At the T-junction with Fetter Lane, turn left.
- At the 'traffic light' T-junction with Fleet Street, turn right.
- Take the first right into Chancery Lane.
- Turn left into Carey Street, then right into Serle Street.
- Turn left at the corner of Lincoln's Inn Fields to run along their south side.
- Turn right to run up the west side of Lincoln's Inn Fields, then left onto Remnant Street.
- Cross Kingsway at the traffic lights and continue on Great Queen Street.

- Cross Drury Lane into Long Acre; when Long Acre becomes one-way against you, turn right onto Endell Street.
- Turn left onto Shorts Gardens.
- Turn right by the Cambridge Theatre Stage Door onto Mercer Street and up the cobbled hill to Seven Dials.
- Take the second exit from Seven Dials to take Earlham Street to Cambridge Circus.
- Go through the modal filter and dismount to walk across Shaftesbury Avenue and then Charing Cross Road, to put you in front of the red-brick Palace Theatre.
- Continue into Romilly Street with The Spice of Life pub on your right.
- At the T-junction with Dean Street turn right, then dismount to turn left and walk into one-way Old Compton Street.
- At the end of Old Compton Street walk down Tisbury Court.
- Turn left on Rupert Street, right on Archer Street and right up Great Windmill Street.
- Go straight on over Brewer Street into Lexington Street, then left into Beak Street.
- At the traffic lights turn right onto Regent Street.
- Turn left down Conduit Street and continue into Bruton Street to Berkeley Square.
- Turn left and go round Berkeley Square to take the fourth (north-west) exit, keeping left to turn into Mount Street with the Porsche showroom on your right.
- As the road bends right, turn left to continue on Mount Street.
- Turn right onto Park Street, then left on Upper Grosvenor Street.
- There is a docking station on your right as you emerge into Park Lane or you can cross over and turn right to dock nearer Hyde Park.

Approximate cycling time

0   1   2   3   4   5 minutes

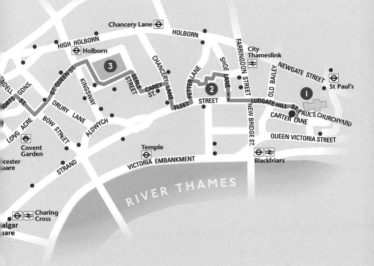

	Shared footpaths or cyclepaths
	Pedestrian areas (dismount)
●	Cycle Hire Docking Station
❶	Place of interest

PLACES OF INTEREST

❶ St Paul's Cathedral
Famously designed by Sir Christopher Wren, the current building is the fourth church to have stood on the site. The scene of many services of national remembrance and the wedding of HRH The Prince of Wales and Lady Diana Spencer in 1981, the cathedral is the resting place of numerous well-known historical figures, such as Admiral Lord Nelson, the Duke of Wellington and Sir Christopher Wren himself. Its dome is the second largest in the world, weighing approximately 65,000 tonnes and contains the Whispering Gallery.

❷ Dr Johnson's House
Samuel Johnson moved to 17 Gough Square to complete his famous dictionary that was eventually published in 1755. Built of brick with a timber frame, the house was saved from falling into disrepair in 1911 by the Liberal MP Cecil Harmsworth. During the Second World War, it operated as a canteen for the Auxiliary Fire Service.

❸ Lincoln's Inn Fields
When the architect Inigo Jones laid out this square – the largest in London – in the 17th century, it was one of the most popular areas in the city. From its early days until the beginning of the 19th century, it was popular with duellists and pickpockets, and physical attacks were not uncommon. These days, visitors can enjoy the lawns or play tennis.

❹ Seven Dials
Lying at the heart of this area is the six-faced monument that was erected to commemorate Thomas Neale's plan for the area – a unique star of seven roads built to form a series of triangles. Now home to a variety of shops and offices, the area was a notorious slum in the 19th century. Agatha Christie commemorated the area in *The Seven Dials Mystery*, and now blue plaques commemorate the old offices of the Beatles' manager Brian Epstein, and the former recording studios of *Monty Python*.

❺ Soho

With a lively mix of restaurants, pubs, bars and offices, Soho's reputation today is somewhat different from the one it enjoyed when it was known for its sex shops. In the 1960s it was popular for its fashion and musical shops in Carnaby Street and Denmark Street, which was called the British Tin Pan Alley. Nowadays Soho is home to London's Chinatown as well as the England Football Association headquarters and numerous media and film production companies and editing suites.

❻ Regent Street

Running from Carlton House at the southern end up to Langham Place, Regent Street has undergone a major redevelopment over the last few years. World-renowned brands attract thousands of visitors each year to what is now a conservation area. These glossy stores are a far cry from the original buildings designed by John Nash in the early 19th century.

Of those, only All Souls Church in Langham Place survives.

❼ Berkeley Square

Few, if any, nightingales sing here now, but the rectangular green space makes a pleasant place to relax. At one time, the square was one of the most desirable addresses in London, but the majority of the buildings are now occupied by offices and businesses. Number 50 was once reputedly the most haunted house in Britain. Various well-known people have lived in the square at various times, including Sir Winston Churchill, Horace Walpole and Robert Clive.

THE SITES
OF SOUTHBANK

You may well need to walk a little on this route around the Blackfriars Bridge section, but it is worth it to appreciate the many attractions of London's South Bank. Whether your tastes turn to music, film, art or theatre, this cultural selection has something for everyone, including spiritual sustenance. Be careful, though, or you may end up 'in clink'.

DISTANCE 5km (3 miles)
PROFILE Flat; the only 'hill' is Westminster Bridge
PICK UP DOCKING STATION Storey's Gate, Westminster
DROP OFF DOCKING STATION Curlew Street, Shad Thames

- Turn left (north) up Storey's Gate.
- At the T-junction, turn right into Great George Street.
- Go straight on along the east side of Parliament Square and up onto Westminster Bridge.
- As you descend from the Bridge, turn left – through the modal filter – into Belvedere Road.
- As you exit from the County Hall buildings – just beyond the modal filter – turn left into Jubilee Gardens.
- Turn right on the Thames Path.
- Go under Waterloo Bridge.
- Walk the narrow section beyond Gabriel's Wharf and continue, passing under Blackfriars Bridge to pass the Millennium footbridge.
- Turn right by The Anchor pub.
- Turn left into Clink Street and continue on Pickfords Wharf.
- Turn right by the *Golden Hinde* sailing ship.
- Turn left into Cathedral Street, bear right and then make a sharp left into Montague Close.

- Pass under London Bridge into Tooley Street.
- At the T-junction turn left to continue on Tooley Street.
- Pass Hays Galleria, then turn left into Battlebridge Lane and right onto the Thames Path.
- Pass under Tower Bridge, through the modal filter, then right into Horselydown Lane and left into Gainsford Street.
- Turn right into Curlew Street to find the docking station.

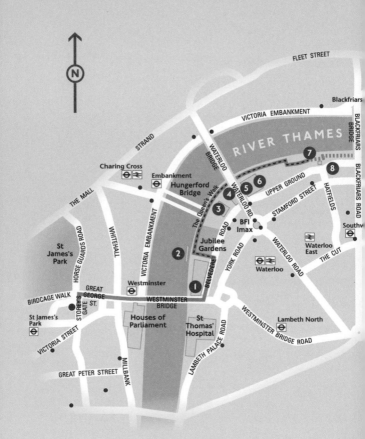

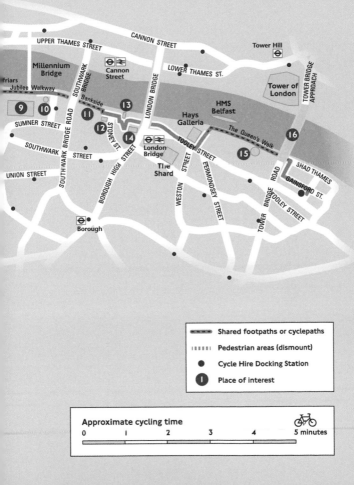

THE SITES OF SOUTHBANK

Shared footpaths or cyclepaths

Pedestrian areas (dismount)

Cycle Hire Docking Station

Place of interest

Approximate cycling time

0   1   2   3   4   5 minutes

PLACES OF INTEREST

❶ Sea Life London Aquarium
Here in what was County Hall, visitors can feed turtles and sharks, enjoy watching the penguins and marvel at a huge range of underwater creatures.

❷ The London Eye
Erected in 1999, this giant Ferris wheel offers some of the best views across London. With a diameter of 120m (394ft), it is also Europe's tallest Ferris wheel.

❸ The Royal Festival Hall
Apart from holding world-class concerts, the Hall also includes the Clore Ballroom, the Saison Poetry Library (the UK's largest collection of modern and contemporary poetry) and a restaurant and café. It was opened in 1951 as part of the Festival of Britain.

❹ The Hayward Gallery
Built in the Brutalist style, the Gallery was named after Sir Isaac Hayward and opened in 1968. It has no permanent collection, but holds several exhibitions

each year, focusing on modern and contemporary art.

❺ BFI Southbank
Formerly known as the National Film Theatre, the building was refurbished to take in what was the Museum of the Moving Image. As well as three cinemas, it is also home to a studio, gallery and médiathèque.

❻ The Royal National Theatre
Built in the 1970s as a permanent home for the National Theatre Company, the NT contains three theatres that offer productions of Shakespeare's plays as well as contemporary works.

❼ Gabriel's Wharf
Enjoy the mix of retail outlets that offer a host of contemporary furnishings, jewellery and ceramics. This is part of this redevelopment instituted by the Coin Street Community Builders.

❽ OXO Tower
Formerly owned by the manufacturers of OXO stock

cubes, the tower was renovated in the 1990s with the restaurant at the top opening in 1996. The rest of the tower is home to a number of design studios and flats, as well as two galleries and shops.

❾ Tate Modern
The nation's collections of British art from 1500 and international modern and contemporary art are showcased in this disused power station. It also holds world-class temporary exhibitions.

❿ Shakespeare's Globe Theatre
Founded by the actor and director Sam Wanamaker, this reconstruction of the original Globe Theatre with its open-air thrust stage, offers performances between May and October and numerous educational programmes through the year.

⓫ The Anchor Pub
Lying on the site of a Roman grave, the pub was probably given its name by the 17th-century brewery owner, Josiah Childs, who supplied goods to the Navy.

⓬ The Clink Prison Museum
Built on the original site of the Clink Prison, one of the oldest prisons in the country and which housed many notorious prisoners, this museum tells the story of the prison and its sorry inmates.

⓭ The *Golden Hinde*
A beautiful reconstruction of the ship that Sir Francis Drake used to circumnavigate the world in 1577–80.

⓮ Southwark Cathedral
The cathedral church of the diocese of Southwark. There has been a church on this site for more than 1,000 years.

⓯ City Hall
Not just home to the Mayor of London and the headquarters of the Greater London Authority, the Foster + Partners-designed hall has a café and is regularly used for exhibitions.

⓰ Tower Bridge
(See page 94.)

GARDENS, PARKS, MONUMENTS & MEMORIALS

It's hard not to take a little pride in London as you wander through Kensington Gardens and Hyde Park, taking in the features that pepper these popular green spaces, and the fine establishments that line the route which continues via Buckingham Palace to Horse Guards Parade and the home of the Prime Minister, Downing Street.

DISTANCE 7km (4⅓ miles)
PROFILE Flat or downhill
PICK UP DOCKING STATION Notting Hill Gate Station, Notting Hill or Black Lion Gate, Kensington Gardens
DROP OFF DOCKING STATION Butler Place, Westminster

- Go the short distance south to Notting Hill Gate and turn left to ride east toward central London.
- (If you don't like riding with car traffic, you can start at Black Lion Gate by Queensway Underground Station.)
- Move left onto the pavement outside Caroline House just before Queensway Underground Station.
- Use the lights to cross the road and enter Kensington Gardens through Black Lion Gate.
- Follow Broad Walk straight ahead and gently down the hill past The Orangery and Kensington Palace on your right.
- Just after the statue of Queen Victoria turn left; the Round Pond is on your left and the Albert Memorial on your right.
- Cross the West Carriage Drive – a road with cars – and turn left on the cycle lane and immediately right onto a straight cycle path with

a cast-iron fence on the right: the Princess of Wales Memorial Fountain and the Serpentine – an artificial lake – are on your left; the sandy horse track of Rotten Row on your right.

- At the end of the path, cross South Carriage Drive and bear left onto the narrow roadway, aiming for the right-hand arch of the colonnaded screen. Apsley House, also known as Number One London, is on your left.
- (A left turn before you leave the park will allow you to ride circuits of the Serpentine – watch out for skaters – or Hyde Park via Speakers Corner.)
- Use the light-controlled crossings to go over first Knightsbridge, then the Hyde Park Corner roundabout. You are aiming for the Wellington Arch, with the sculpture of the angel of peace descending on the chariot of war, on top.
- Pass Wellington Arch and use the light-controlled crossing to get to the top of Constitution Hill.
- You can ride down Constitution Hill on the road or on the cycle path to its left.
- At the bottom of the hill Buckingham Palace is on your right; this is the easiest place to access the space between the palace and the fountains.
- Bear left to ride away from the palace on The Mall.
- You have the choice to ride on the road or on the parallel, motor traffic-free access road, which can be accessed directly from the Constitution Hill cycle path. If you are using the access road, use the light-controlled crossing to go over the bottom of Marlborough Road.
- If you stay on the road, move right to avoid the far left-hand lane at the first set of traffic lights.
- Turn right at end of the park onto Horse Guards Parade. (The 30 steps up to your left – where you turn – lead to Waterloo Place and The Duke of York's Column, where there is a docking station.)
- From here you have no choice but to ride on the road. Traffic is usually polite on these well-surfaced and policed avenues, so it is a good place to start sharing space with motor traffic.

- At the end of Horse Guards Parade, turn right at the T-junction onto Birdcage Walk.
- At the first light-controlled crossing, stop on the left and walk through the gates to exit the park.
- Once through the gates, you can remount and continue straight ahead in Queen Anne's Gate.
- Turn right outside St James's Park Underground Station onto Petty France.
- Turn left onto Palmer Street.
- Go straight on at the T-junction with great care, into the narrow alley still called Palmer Street; walking may be necessary. Find the docking station in Butler Place.

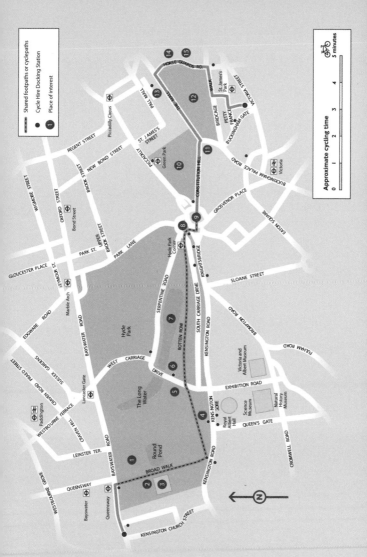

PLACES OF INTEREST

① Kensington Gardens
Much of the development of the gardens is due to various queens, not least Queen Caroline (the wife of George II) who was responsible for the creation of the Serpentine and the Long Water. It contains many statues, including Dr Edward Jenner and Peter Pan, and the Elfin Oak carving.

② The Orangery
Queen Anne built this beautiful 18th-century building for court entertainment; visitors can now enjoy breakfast and lunches here.

③ Kensington Palace
Based on the original Jacobean house known as Nottingham House, the palace was designed by Sir Christopher Wren to house King William and Queen Mary, and is still the home of members of the royal family. The palace is open to visitors and there are regular special exhibitions.

④ The Albert Memorial
Designed by George Gilbert Scott, this memorial to Prince Albert was unveiled in 1872. Now fully restored, the gleaming gold statue draws the eye to the memorial's highly ornate design.

⑤ The Serpentine Gallery
A Grade II-listed, former tea pavilion, this world-renowned gallery is dedicated to exhibitions of contemporary art, architecture and design. It is complemented by the Zaha Hadid-designed Serpentine Sackler Gallery, which opened in 2013.

⑥ The Princess of Wales Memorial Fountain
The fountain was opened in 2004. Designed by Kathryn Gustaffson, it consists of an oval stream bed made from Cornish granite.

⑦ The Serpentine
This 16-ha (40-acre) lake was a focal point of the Great Exhibition in 1851. Visitors can enjoy boating on the lake or relax at the nearby restaurants.

⑧ Apsley House
Also known as Number One,

London, this was the former home of the Duke of Wellington, and contains more than 3,000 works of art.

❾ Wellington Arch
Built in 1825–27, the arch was originally meant to stand outside Buckingham Palace. It was moved to its current site in 1883–85.

❿ Green Park
Once renowned for highwaymen and thieves, the smallest of the Royal Parks (19ha/47 acres) contains the RAF Bomber Command Memorial and the Canada Memorial.

⓫ Buckingham Palace
Containing 775 rooms, the palace has been used by monarchs as their official residence since 1837. Open to the public in the summer, the palace holds numerous priceless works of art.

⓬ St James's Park
With an ornamental lake, this 23-ha (57-acre) oasis was landscaped on the orders of James I. Charles II opened it to the public, and in the 17th and 18th century it was used for grazing cows.

⓭ The Institute of Contemporary Arts
Founded by a group of artists in 1946, the ICA moved to Nash House in 1968, where it holds exhibitions, talks and debates. It has also been the venue of debut solo exhibitions by artists such as Damien Hirst, Steve McQueen and Luc Tuymans.

⓮ Horse Guards Parade
Best known as the venue for the annual Trooping the Colour ceremony, this parade ground is surrounded by government buildings, such as the Old Admiralty and the Foreign and Commonwealth Office.

⓯ Downing Street
This 17th-century street was built by Sir George Downing. Number 10 is the official home of the Prime Minister; number 11 of the Chancellor of the Exchequer; and number 12 of the Chief Whip.

LONDON'S BURNING

17th-century London is highlighted by a tour that begins along the spread of the Great Fire of London in 1666. But the route carries on to take in some of London's most remarkable buildings and a moving memorial to the end of the slave trade before finishing at the Bloody Tower.

DISTANCE 6km (3¾ miles)

PROFILE Technical riding on narrow cobbled lanes and courts; some short hills

PICK UP DOCKING STATION Monument, Monument Street

DROP OFF DOCKING STATION Crosswall, Tower

- Set off up the hill towards the Monument. Cross the footpath by the Monument with care and continue up Monument Street. The monument marks the starting point of the Great Fire of London.
- At the top of Monument Street, dismount and walk a few metres south – towards London Bridge – on the pavement of King William Street.
- When the barrier in the centre of the road ends, cross carefully on foot.
- Turn away from the river and turn left to descend into Arthur Street.
- Turn sharp right into Martin Street.
- Turn immediately left into Laurence Pountney Hill. Take care and be polite; you may have to walk in places.
- Go straight on over Suffolk Lane into Gophir Lane.
- Turn right on Bush Lane and up to Cannon Street.
- Turn left on Cannon Street and – immediately after the station – left again into Dowgate Hill.
- Turn right onto Cloak Lane.
- Go straight on over Queen Street into Great St Thomas the Apostle and continue into Great Trinity Lane.

- Go left on the semi-circular road, then left again onto Queen Victoria Street.
- Turn right into Friday Street and left on Cannon Street.
- At the wooden bollard on the left – by the bus stop and grand stone water fountain – turn left up onto the footpath and then right down the line of Carter Lane, with the National Firefighters Memorial on your left, and the City of London Information Centre on your right.
- Continue over Godliman Street to stay on Carter Lane.
- At the T-junction, turn left on Black Friars Lane and go down to Queen Victoria Street.
- Dismount and turn right on the footpath under the railway bridge. At the corner cross New Bridge Street on foot to continue straight on into Watergate marked 'No Entry Except Cycles'. You have just crossed the River Fleet as the Great Fire of London did in 1666.
- Bear right into Kingscote Street, and at the T-junction, turn left onto Tudor Street.
- At the gates of the Temple – the western limit of the Great Fire – turn right up Temple Lane.
- Bear right, then turn left into Lombard Lane, bear right into Pleydell Street, then left – at the T-junction – into Bouverie Street.
- Turn left at the T-junction onto Fleet Street, then right up Fetter Lane.
- At the statue of John Wilkes, turn left into Breams Buildings, and immediately right to stay on Fetter Lane.
- Cross the westbound carriageway of Holborn and turn right on the far side to head east towards the City.
- Go straight on at the traffic lights; you are re-crossing the River Fleet on Holborn Viaduct.
- Turn left onto Giltspur Street.
- Pass the Golden Boy of Pye Corner at first floor level on your left, on the corner of Cock Lane. The Golden Boy marks the furthest north-west limit of the Great Fire.
- At the top of Giltspur Street, go through the modal filter and right on curving West Smithfield.

- Turn right onto Cloth Fair, then continue onto Middle Street.
- At the T-junction, turn left on Cloth Street, then right onto Long Lane.
- At the traffic lights, turn right onto Aldersgate Street.
- Take the first exit at the Museum of London roundabout into London Wall.
- Stop on the left and you will see the remains of the old wall; this is the area of Cripple Gate, where the Great Fire reached the city walls.
- Walk across London Wall – through the rough concrete blocks in the centre – to go south through the modal filter on Noble Street. There are more remains of the city walls on your right.
- Turn left onto Gresham Street. Pass the Guildhall on your left.
- Continue straight on on Lothbury; the large building to your right is the Bank of England.
- When the road bears right, continue straight on into Throgmorton Street.
- At the T-junction, turn right on Old Broad Street.
- Turn left onto Threadneedle Street.
- Turn right on Bishopsgate and – on the top of Cornhill – left onto Leadenhall Street.
- Turn right into Lime Street, pass through the modal filters with care, and then turn left onto Fenchurch Avenue.
- Turn right down Fen Court, pass the sculpture 'Gilt of Cain'; you may have to walk here.
- Turn left on Fenchurch Street.
- Turn right onto Lloyd's Avenue.
- Go right at the T-junction with Crutched Friars, and immediately left to find the docking station in Crosswall.
- The Tower of London marks the eastern limit of the Great Fire. The Tower was saved by blowing up adjacent houses with gunpowder to provide a fire break.

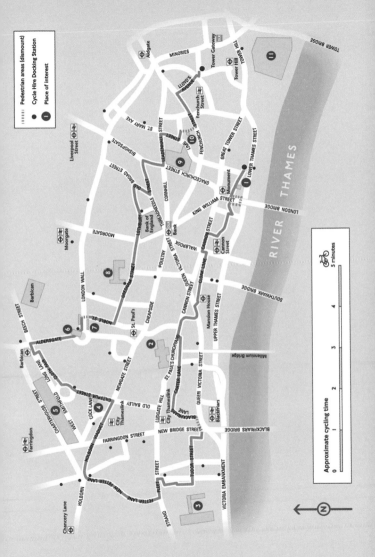

LONDON'S BURNING

PLACES OF INTEREST

❶ The Monument
Built between 1671 and 1677 to
commemorate the Great Fire of
London that started in a baker's
house in Pudding Lane on 2
September 1666, the Monument
was designed by Sir Christopher
Wren and Dr Robert Hooke, and
has a viewing gallery at the top.
It is 62m (202ft) high, which is
the exact distance between it
and the site of the original fire.

❷ St Paul's Cathedral
(See page 22.)

❸ The Temple
Consisting of the Inner and
Middle Temples (two of the Inns
of Court), this area teems with
London's legal life. Named after
the area's connection to the
Knights Templar, whose church
stands to the north, the two
Temples are extra-parochial
areas, meaning that they are
not under the governance of
the City of London Corporation,
nor do they fall under the
ecclesiastical jurisdiction
of the Bishop of London.

❹ The Golden Boy of Pye Corner
Made of wood and covered in
gold, this small statue of a boy
marks the spot where the
Great Fire of London stopped.
Deliberately made to look chubby
to warn against the sin of gluttony,
the statue was originally placed
on the façade of a pub called
The Fortune of War, which stood
on the same site.

❺ Smithfield
Best known for its meat market
that has been here since medieval
times, this area is also home to
many institutions, including St
Batholomew's Hospital and
the Charterhouse, a former
Carthusian monastery. Street
names highlight the area's
association with livestock, but it
has also been the venue for some
notable executions, such as that
of Wat Tyler, who led the Peasants'
Revolt in 1381.

❻ Museum of London
Based on the original collections
of the Guildhall and the former
London Museum, the museum

opened in the 1970s. The collections offer a fascinating insight into London's social and cultural history.

7 London's Walls

Not much remains of the original wall, but it was one of the last major construction projects undertaken by the Romans. Built mainly from Kentish ragstone, the wall was about 3.2 km (2 miles) long and a ditch about 1.8m (6ft) deep was dug in front of the outer wall eventually becoming London's main rubbish site. Most of the wall was destroyed in the Great Fire of London.

8 Guildhall

The current Guildhall was built between 1411 and 1440 and stands on the site of a Roman amphitheatre, some of which can be seen in the basement of the Guildhall Art Gallery. Beneath the Guildhall lies the largest medieval crypt in London, while the Victorian Gothic-style Old Library and Livery Hall are Grade II listed. The trial of Lady Jane Grey took place in the hall and it was also the venue for Frederic Chopin's last public performance in 1848.

9 Leadenhall Market

Film buffs will be familiar with this covered market, as it has appeared in a number of films, such as *Harry Potter and the Philosopher's Stone* and *Lara Croft: Tomb Raider*, as well as pop videos. Dating back to the 14th century, the market would have been at the centre of Roman London. Refurbished at the beginning of the 1990s, it is a Grade II-listed building.

10 The Gilt of Cain

Michael Visocchi and Lemn Sissay's moving sculpture commemorates the abolition in 1807 of the slave trade across the Atlantic. The granite monument is inscribed with part of Lemn Sissay's poem 'Gilt of Cain', which makes reference to both the City's Stock Exchange trading floor and the Old Testament.

11 Tower of London
(See page 94.)

THE WEST BANK
OF THE FLEET RIVER

This route traverses part of the River Fleet's underground course, taking you through the old 'Convent' Garden and Bloomsbury, to the Victorian Gothic splendour of St Pancras.

DISTANCE 4km (2½ miles)
PROFILE Very gently uphill
PICK UP DOCKING STATION Waterloo Station
DROP OFF DOCKING STATION Belgrove Street, King's Cross

- Roll down Station Road on the cycle track and turn right onto York Road at the light-controlled crossing.
- Take the first major exit from the roundabout going up onto Waterloo Bridge. Go ahead to cross The Strand into Wellington Street.
- Turn right onto Tavistock Street, then left onto Catherine Street.
- Turn right on Russell Street, turn left on Drury Lane, and then turn right onto Great Queen Street.
- Cross the Kingsway at the traffic lights and continue into Remnant Street and along the north side of Lincoln's Inn Fields.
- Turn left at the T-junction onto Newman's Row, then dismount and walk straight ahead onto Great Turnstile.
- Remount and turn left on Holborn and immediately right into Red Lion Street. At the traffic lights on Theobald's Road go straight ahead.
- At the top of Lamb's Conduit Street turn left, and then turn right onto Lansdowne Terrace. Take the third exit at the roundabout into Brunswick Square, which becomes Judd Street. Go straight on at the traffic-light crossroads, then right onto Cromer Street.
- Turn left onto Whidborne Street, signposted King's Cross.
- Turn right at the T-junction with Argyle Street, then left onto Argyle Square, which becomes Belgrove Street; the docking station is on the right.

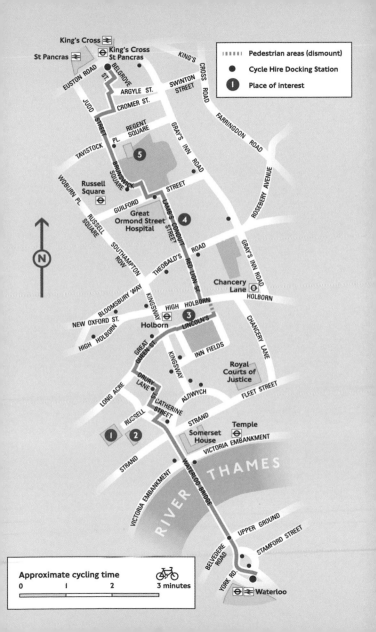

PLACES OF INTEREST

❶ Covent Garden Market
Originally part of the Bedford estate, and until the 1970s the home of London's principal wholesale fruit and vegetable market, the area is now filled with luxury shops, small boutiques and stalls selling artisan crafts and jewellery. The piazza is regularly filled with street performers and offers access to the nearby Royal Opera House. On the south side you will also find Jubilee Market, which sells a variety of goods depending on the day of the week.

❷ London Transport Museum
With more than 450,000 items in its collections, including examples of trams, buses, taxis and Tube trains, there is plenty to see. Housed in what was the Flower Market, visitors can examine photographs and posters and watch films about the development of London's transport system.

❸ Sir John Soane Museum
Soane was Professor of Architecture at the Royal Academy at the beginning of the 19th century and his former home contains his collection of art, sculpture and architectural casts and models. Highlights of the collection include Hogarth's *A Rake's Progress* and the sarcophagus of the Pharaoh Seti I.

❹ Bikefix
Specialising in folding bikes, this shop is a must for bike enthusiasts, with its selection of equipment – from all kinds of bikes to accessories – and its repair shop.

❺ Coram's Fields and The Foundling Museum
The fields lie on the site of the former Foundling Hospital that was established by Captain Thomas Coram, and adults are allowed into them only if accompanied by a child aged 16 or under. The nearby Foundling Museum contains the hospital's art collection as well as the Gerald Coke Handel Collection. Within the park, children can enjoy play areas and games galore.

INLAND CRUISING

Based on the River Lea Navigation, this route takes in some magnificent facilities in the newly developed Millennium and Queen Elizabeth II Olympic Parks, and visits some of East London's lesser known but fascinating watery developments that have been repurposed from their previous industrial usage.

DISTANCE 10km (6¼ miles)
PROFILE No hills; some short, steep narrow sections by the locks on the Hertford Cut
PICK UP DOCKING STATION The Green Bridge, Mile End
DROP OFF DOCKING STATION The Green Bridge, Mile End

- You can break the route into shorter sections by using the docking stations at Gunmaker's Lane, Old Ford or Stainsby Road, Poplar.
- Ride west (left) on the Mile End Road.
- Cross the road – walk if necessary – to enter Whitman Road beside the New Globe Tavern. If you cross the canal bridge, you've gone too far.
- Keep left to join the towpath of the Regent's Canal.
- Slow down and ring your bell when passing under bridges. Be prepared to stop. Pedestrians have priority on all the waterway paths.
- On top of the bridge that crosses the mouth of the Hertford Cut, turn right to double back and descend to follow the Hertford Cut towpath. If you reach Old Ford Lock, you've gone too far.
- Take care as you descend past locks on this section: the paths are steep and narrow and run close to the water. Walk if necessary.
- At the T-junction with the River Lea Navigation, follow the path to the left and up onto White Post Lane.
- Cross the Navigation on the bridge – the Olympic Park is straight ahead – then turn right to descend to the Navigation towpath.
- Follow the towpath, then – after going under the second railway bridge – cross the Navigation on the new footbridge and descend to go

under Stratford High Street on the new floating path.

- Turn left to cross the Navigation on the road bridge entrance to Three Mill Island.
- Continue on the Navigation towpath to Bow Locks and walk over the concrete bridge. Remount and continue to take the floating path under the bridge and join the towpath of the Limehouse Cut.
- When the Cut emerges at the Limehouse Basin, cross the Cut on the footbridge and then follow the north side of the Basin to find the mouth of the Regent's Canal.
- Follow the towpath and – just before the brick arch bridge, Number 58 – turn right into the parallel park and continue to find the docking station on the Mile End Road.

PLACES OF INTEREST

❶ Millennium Park
(See page 87.)

❷ Victoria Park
London's oldest public park, it is often called the People's Park and covers 86ha (213 acres), bordering Bethnal Green, Hackney and Bow. The park has offered space for sports and relaxation since 1845 when it was landscaped by the architect Sir James Pennethorne, a student of John Nash. At one time, the park was used for political rallies, but in recent years it has hosted concerts and was used as a venue during the 2012 Olympics.

❸ Queen Elizabeth II Olympic Park
(See page 87.)

❹ Fish Island
So-called because of the piscatorial nature of its street names, this area has so far avoided massive redevelopment. But while the 'industrial' look has been maintained, the buildings' usage has been converted to the extent that the former warehouses and factories are now residential flats and studios for a huge community of artists, designers and craftsmen and women. There is still also a link with fish since it is also the site of H. Forman & Son, the world's oldest producer of smoked salmon.

❺ Three Mill Island
Formed by the Prescott Channel, a former flood relief channel, the island has been the site of mills since Saxon times. It still boasts four mills, including the Grade-I-listed House Mill, the world's biggest tidal mill, and the Grade II-listed Clock Mill. The latter is part of the 4-ha (10-acre) 3 Mills Studios. With the open green space of Three Mills Green and Wild Kingdom, a play space for children, the island offers excellent facilities to sit and unwind.

❻ Limehouse Basin
(See page 95.)

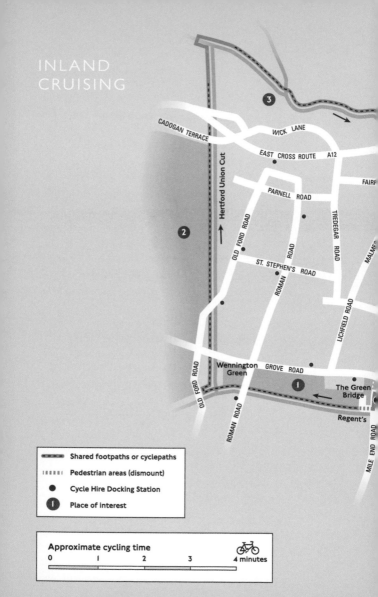

INLAND CRUISING

CADOGAN TERRACE

WICK LANE

EAST CROSS ROUTE A12

PARNELL ROAD

Hertford Union Cut

Old Ford Road

ST. STEPHEN'S ROAD

ROMAN ROAD

TREDEGAR ROAD

LICHFIELD ROAD

FAIRF

MALMES

OLD FORD ROAD

Wennington Green

GROVE ROAD

The Green Bridge

ROMAN ROAD

Regent's

MILE END ROAD

━━━ Shared footpaths or cyclepaths

ııııı Pedestrian areas (dismount)

● Cycle Hire Docking Station

❶ Place of interest

Approximate cycling time

| 0 | 1 | 2 | 3 | 4 minutes |

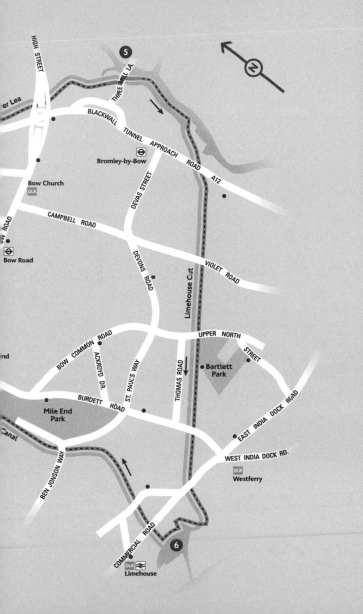

GREEN TO GREEN BY OLD MARY-LE-BONE

If you can leave the delights of Hyde Park, take a trip to another of the glorious Royal Parks via old Mary-le-bone with its excellent shops, and enjoy some culture along the way at the Wallace Collection.

DISTANCE 5km (3 miles), you can go further by adding a circuit(s) of either park
PROFILE Very gently uphill
PICK UP DOCKING STATION Triangle Car Park, Hyde Park
DROP OFF DOCKING STATION The Tennis Courts, Regent's Park or Park Road (Baker Street), Regent's Park

- Ride down to the ornamental lake – The Serpentine – and continue east along Serpentine Road with the water on your right. Serpentine Road, also known as The Beach, is popular with skaters; they can turn suddenly and have no brakes, so take care.
- Continue on Serpentine Road beyond the lake and, before it exits onto South Carriage Drive, turn sharp left, uphill, to pass the statue of Achilles.
- Continue north, with Park Lane parallel on your right, to Speakers' Corner.
- As you approach the corner of the Park, bear left.
- Pass the docking station, then turn right to cross North Carriage Drive onto the cycle track to Stanhope Gate, crossing Hyde Park Place to enter Stanhope Place.
- At the corner of Connaught Square, turn right into Seymour Street.
- Cross Edgware Road and continue on Seymour Street.
- Turn left into Portman Square, then right to continue along the north side of the Square and ahead into Fitzhardinge Street.

- Turn left and right and right to go round Manchester Square; the Wallace Collection is on your left.
- Turn left to exit Manchester Square on Hinde Street.
- Turn left onto Thayer Street and when the road becomes one-way – against you – the simplest thing is to dismount and walk the three short shop-fronts; Thayer Street then becomes Marylebone High Street.
- Turn left into Paddington Street, right into Nottingham Place, right into Nottingham Street and – finally – left to rejoin Marylebone High Street.
- The Garden of Rest is on your left with a docking station (Beaumont Street, Marylebone) conveniently opposite if you want to take a break.
- At the junction with Marylebone Road, dismount and cross the road using the light-controlled crossing on your right.
- Ride the first section of Macfarren Place, walk the very short, one-way section, then turn left at the T-junction onto York Terrace East.
- Turn right onto York Gate, go straight on across the Outer Circle onto York Bridge.
- Cross the ornamental bridge; the docking station is half-hidden behind a hedge on your right.
- If the Park is closed, or you don't want to visit it, there is an alternative docking station at Park Street.
- From York Gate do not go ahead into York Bridge. Instead turn left on the Outer Circle and continue to take the first left into Clarence Gate. As you double back into Baker Street the docking station is on your right.

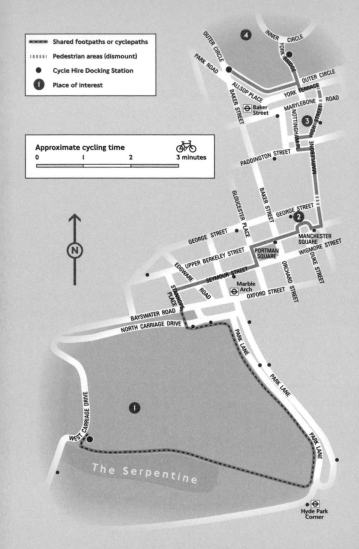

GREEN TO GREEN BY
OLD MARY-LE-BONE

PLACES OF INTEREST

❶ Hyde Park

This 142-ha (350-acre) park was first opened to the public by King Charles I in 1637. It has been at the heart of London and national life for hundreds of years and contains many significant memorials. The site of the Great Exhibition in 1851, Hyde Park has hosted rallies, concerts and sports events, including some of the 2012 Olympics. For a little cerebral stimulus on a Sunday morning, stop off at Speakers' Corner near Marble Arch, and listen to the amateur orators on their chosen topic.

❷ The Wallace Collection

Based in Hertford House, the collection consists of the works of art gathered together by Sir Richard Wallace and the first four Marquises of Hertford. Highlights include Gainsborough's *The Laughing Cavalier* and Fragonard's *Girl on a Swing*, but there are many other works as well as beautiful examples of Sèvres porcelain and a fascinating collection of miniatures. Enjoy a meal in the glass-roofed courtyard that houses the Wallace Restaurant.

❸ The Memorial Garden of Rest

Commemorating the parish church of Marylebone that was demolished in 1949, this mainly paved garden was opened in 1951 on the same site. The surrounding walls are full of plaques to the great and the good connected to the parish, including Charles Wesley, who was buried at the church in 1788.

❹ Regent's Park

With nearly 160ha (395 acres) of space, this Royal Park offers plenty for everyone, housing as it does the Open Air Theatre, London Zoo and sports facilities that cover almost 40.5ha (100 acres). Queen Mary's Gardens hold London's largest collection of roses (approximately 12,000), as well as a national collection of delphiniums. The park is also the venue for numerous events throughout the year, including the Frieze Art Fair.

CRAWLING CAMDEN

Roam around the railway hub of old Somers Town and the country's greatest repository of publications at the British Library, to the colour and exuberance of Camden and Kentish Town, and back to the bustle of London's newest grand square via the tranquillity of the Regent's Canal.

DISTANCE 7km (4⅓ miles)
PROFILE No hills; some gentle climbing
PICK UP DOCKING STATION Cartwright Gardens, Bloomsbury
DROP OFF DOCKING STATION Belgrove Street, King's Cross

- Ride north on Cartwright Gardens with the gardens and tennis courts on your left and continue as Cartwright Gardens becomes Mabledon Place.
- At the traffic light T-junction, turn right onto Euston Road and immediately left into Ossulston Street. The British Library is on your right.
- Turn right onto the Polygon Road cycle path.
- Turn left on Purchese Street and continue into Goldington Street, then left into Goldington Crescent.
- Use the light-controlled crossing to go on up the cycle track parallel to Royal College Street.
- Turn right onto Georgiana Street and then left on the cycle track parallel to St Pancras Way.
- At the traffic lights at the end of the cycle track, turn right into Agar Grove.
- At the next junction, fork left onto the cycle path.
- Turn right onto Rochester Square.
- At the T-junction, turn right on Camden Road and immediately left onto Rochester Road.

- Walk across the footpath by the Greek Orthodox Church and turn right on Kentish Town Road.
- Take the first left into Kelly Street.
- At the end of Kelly Street cross the footpath and turn right on Castlehaven Road.
- Turn left at the T-junction on Prince of Wales Road, then straight ahead past the Fiddlers Elbow music venue.
- Turn left on Crogsland Road.
- Turn left onto Chalk Farm Road; Marine Ices is to the right.
- When the Chalk Farm Road becomes one way, dismount and walk up to the canal bridge, and left onto the Regent's Canal towpath in Camden Lock market.
- Follow the towpath south-east down towards King's Cross.
- Turn left to bump up the wide steps leading up to the fountains of Granary Square.
- Go over the canal on the new bridge, and then cross Goods Way into King's Boulevard.
- Turn left on Pancras Road, and cross the Euston Road at the traffic lights to find the docking station on Belgrove Street.

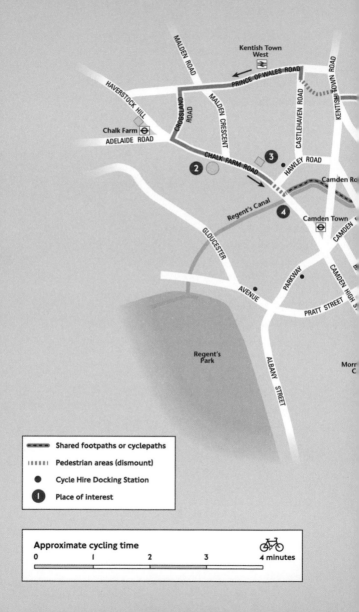

Kentish Town
West

MALDEN ROAD

PRINCE OF WALES ROAD

HAVERSTOCK HILL

KENTISH TOWN ROAD

CROGSLAND ROAD

MALDEN CRESCENT

CASTLEHAVEN ROAD

Chalk Farm

ADELAIDE ROAD

CHALK FARM ROAD

2

3

HAWLEY ROAD

Camden Ro

4

Camden Town

Regent's Canal

CAMDEN

GLOUCESTER

PARKWAY

CAMDEN HIGH S

PRATT STREET

AVENUE

Regent's
Park

ALBANY STREET

Morr
C

- ▰▰▰ Shared footpaths or cyclepaths
- ꟼꟼꟼꟼ Pedestrian areas (dismount)
- ● Cycle Hire Docking Station
- **❶** Place of interest

Approximate cycling time

0   1   2   3   4 minutes

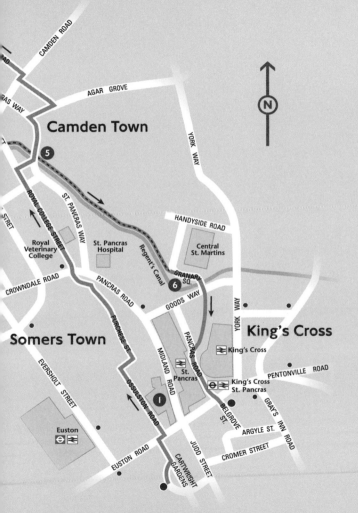

N

Camden Road

Agar Grove

...as Way

Camden Town

5

Royal College Street

St. Pancras Way

Royal Veterinary College

St. Pancras Hospital

Regent's Canal

Crowndale Road

Pancras Road

Handyside Road

Central St. Martins

Granary Sq.

6

Goods Way

York Way

Purchese St.

Somers Town

Midland Road

St. Pancras

Ossulston Road

King's Cross

King's Cross

York Way

Pentonville Road

King's Cross St. Pancras

Gray's Inn Road

Eversholt Street

Euston

1

Belgrove St.

Argyle St.

Euston Road

Judd Street

Cromer Street

Cartwright Gardens

PLACES OF INTEREST

❶ The British Library
The national library of the UK and the world's largest library in terms of the number of catalogued items (170 million plus), the British Library holds manuscripts that date back as far as 2000BC. The St Pancras site holds regular exhibitions based on the library's collections. Items include manuscripts by Leonardo da Vinci, Geoffrey Chaucer and Charlotte Brontë.

❷ The Roundhouse
This former engine repair shop became a centre for the arts in the mid-1960s thanks to the playwright Arnold Wesker. Performers included Jimi Hendrix, Pink Floyd, Vanessa Redgrave and Helen Mirren. Closed for some time, it reopened in 2006 and now includes the Paul Hamlyn Roundhouse Studios.

❸ Marine Ices
Established in 1931 by Gaetano Mansi, this ice-cream parlour still uses the original recipes that Mansi brought with him from Italy.

❹ Camden Lock Market
Still going strong after 40 years, the market began by focusing on selling art and crafts, but you will now find some great fast-food stalls, as well as second-hand books, clothes and jewellery.

❺ Regent's Canal
Named after the Prince Regent (later King George IV), the canal was built to link up the Grand Union Canal and the Thames at Limehouse. The 13.8-km (8.6-mile) waterway is a popular route for cyclists and has even given its name to a musical that celebrates its construction. Beneath part of the towpath lies a network of 400kV electric cables that form part of the National Grid.

❻ Granary Square
Sit and watch the boats pass by on Regent's Canal, enjoy a meal, or watch the display created by 1,000 individually lit fountains that can also be choreographed.

A MAGIC PORTAL
ON THE SURREY SIDE

Cross from the Middlesex side of the Thames to the delights of the south side, with a route that takes you from the seat of government past some of the city's most diverse theatrical venues, intriguing historical sites and a foodie heaven.

DISTANCE 4km (2½ miles)
PROFILE Lambeth Bridge is the only 'hill'
PICK UP DOCKING STATION Abingdon Green, Great College Street
DROP OFF DOCKING STATION Hop Exchange, The Borough

- Emerge from Great College Street onto Millbank and ride west, away from the Palace of Westminster.
- At the roundabout take the first exit up onto Lambeth Bridge. At the roundabout take the second exit to go over into Lambeth Road.
- Go under the railway bridge, then left onto Hercules Road.
- Turn left onto Kennington Road and immediately fork right at the traffic lights into Baylis Road with Lambeth North Station on your right.
- The back of Waterloo Station is on your left. (A left turn takes you into Lower Marsh.) At the traffic lights go straight on into The Cut with The Old Vic on your right; at the next lights go over into Union Street.
- At the traffic lights on Southwark Bridge Road, go straight on through the modal filter by the Island Café to continue on Union Street.
- At the T-junction with Borough High Street, turn left.
- When Borough High Street forks, take the smaller road to the left of the War Memorial. (The George Inn is ahead on the right of the right fork, and the Old Operating Theatre on St Thomas Street a right turn just past the George.)
- Turn left on Southwark Street (Borough Market is ahead up Stoney Street); the docking station is on your left.

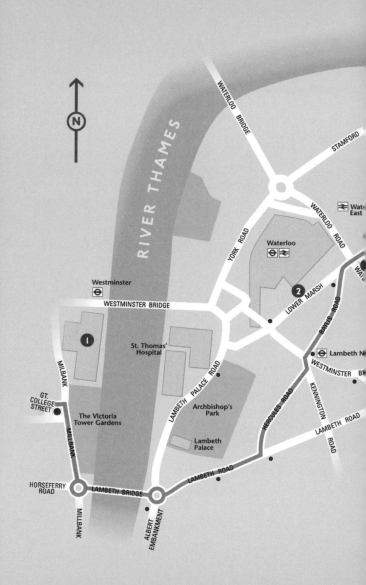

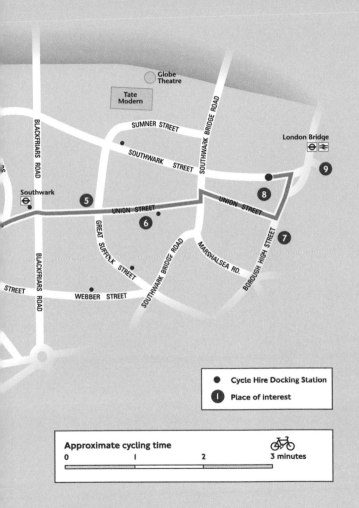

Globe
Theatre

Tate
Modern

SUMNER STREET

SOUTHWARK STREET

SOUTHWARK BRIDGE ROAD

London Bridge

Southwark

5

UNION STREET

UNION STREET

8

9

6

BLACKFRIARS ROAD

GREAT SUFFOLK STREET

SOUTHWARK BRIDGE ROAD

MARSHALSEA RD.

BOROUGH HIGH STREET

7

BLACKFRIARS ROAD

STREET

WEBBER STREET

● Cycle Hire Docking Station

1 Place of interest

Approximate cycling time

0   1   2   3 minutes

A MAGIC PORTAL
ON THE SURREY SIDE

PLACES OF INTEREST

❶ The Palace of Westminster
A palace has stood on this site since the early 11th century. In 1834, a fire started on 16 October, destroying huge swathes of the palace. The architect Charles Barry won the 1835 competition to design the restoration. He was aided by Augustus Welby Pugin, who undertook much of the Gothic-style interior design that is now so renowned. Covering 3.2ha (8 acres), the palace has 1,100 rooms and 5km (3 miles) of corridors. The famous bell, Big Ben, is housed in the Clock Tower at the north end of the palace. The State Opening of Parliament takes place on the first day of a new parliamentary session, or just after a general election.

❷ Lower Marsh Market
There has been a market on this site since the early 19th century, when the marsh that existed here was drained at the time of the building of Waterloo Bridge. At its height, the market stretched from Blackfriars to Vauxhall.

❸ The Old Vic
Best known as the original base of the National Theatre founded by Sir Laurence Olivier in 1963, the Old Vic was originally called the Royal Coburg Theatre when it opened in 1818. The patronage of Queen Victoria's mother led to the name by which it is now known. Many famous actors have performed here, and between 2003 and 2015, American actor Kevin Spacey served as Artistic Director.

❹ The Young Vic
The Young Vic Company was established in 1946 as an offshoot of the Old Vic Theatre School by the director George Devine. The company folded in 1948 but in 1969 Frank Dunlop took up the role as founder-director of the Young Vic Theatre. Refurbished between 2004 and 2006, it has given many budding actors a chance to showcase their talents, and has also hosted musicians, such as The Who.

❺ Union Theatre and Café
Once a paper warehouse, the Union Theatre owes its existence to Sasha Regan, who established it in 1998. Housed in the old railway arches, it has a welcoming café and has gained a reputation for excellent musical productions.

❻ The Jerwood Space
Set in an old Victorian school, this arts venue began life in 1998 thanks to the Jerwood Foundation. It offers facilities for both young and established dance and theatre companies to develop their productions. It also houses a gallery.

❼ The George Inn
Tucked away in a cobbled yard, this quaint public house is the last galleried inn in London. Although owned by the National Trust, it is leased to a private company. This famous coaching inn would house travellers in the upper storeys while customers enjoyed the bars downstairs, and it is possible that Shakespeare was a visitor. Charles Dickens certainly came, using the inn in his book *Little Dorrit*.

❽ Borough Market
This popular market has become a foodie heaven, offering a wide range of organic produce. The area has played host to markets since the 11th century. Many stallholders produce the food that they sell.

❾ The Old Operating Theatre Museum and Herb Garret
This operating theatre was 'rediscovered' in 1957 and reopened to the public in 1962. It is situated in the garret of St Thomas' Church, which stands on the original site of St Thomas' Hospital. Used to dry medicinal herbs, the garret was converted into an operating theatre in 1822. All the patients treated here were women who had to endure operations without anaesthetics and in full view of an audience.

BERMONDSEY SPA & THE ROTHERHITHE COAST

From the revitalised streets of 'Biscuit Town' via the redevelopment of Surrey Docks to 'old Rotherhythe' from where the *Mayflower* once sailed, this route will take you past some of London's newest developments and one of its greatest engineering feats.

DISTANCE 6km (3¾ miles)

PROFILE No hills

PICK UP DOCKING STATION Bermondsey Street, Bermondsey

DROP OFF DOCKING STATION Curlew Street, Shad Thames

- Ride south – away from the junction with Abbey Street – on Bermondsey Street, passing the Marigold Bar on your right.
- Bear right on Bermondsey Street to reach the traffic-light controlled crossing on Tower Bridge Road. Go straight on into Grange Road.
- Fork left onto Spa Road with the green open space of Bermondsey Spa Gardens on your right.
- Pass Bermondsey Town Hall on your left and go under the railway bridge.
- Turn right at the T-junction – St James Church and churchyard are on your left – onto Thurland Road.
- Turn left at the T-junction onto Dockley Road.
- Turn right at the T-junction onto St James's Road.
- Turn left onto Webster Road.
- Turn left at the T-junction onto Clements Road.
- Turn right at the T-junction onto Southwark Park Road.
- Turn left to enter Southwark Park through Jamaica Gate.
- At the café bear left to exit the park into Gomm Road.
- Turn left at the T-junction onto Lower Road and immediately right at the traffic lights into Surrey Quays Road.

- Pass the inverted pyramid of Canada Water Library on your right, then immediately turn right to cross the pedestrian area towards Canada Water.
- Immediately before the wooden bridge, turn left to follow the ornamental canal, Albion Channel.
- Turn left up the cobbled ramp into Albatross Way, signposted 'Rotherhithe'.
- Go straight on over Needleman Street.
- Cross Deal Porter Street and go down the ramp to bear right into Swann Road.
- Cross Albion Street, then Brunel Road with The Adam and Eve pub on your left.
- Turn left at the T-junction onto Rotherhithe Street.
- Pass the Brunel Museum on your left.
- After the narrow cobbled section of Rotherhithe Street, turn left onto Elephant Lane.
- By The Ship pub, turn right onto the dual-use cycle track.
- Follow the path into Kings Stairs Gardens, then bear right to reach the riverfront.
- Continue upstream on Bermondsey Wall East.
- Turn left into Bevington Street.
- Turn right into Chambers Street.
- Turn left onto George Row at the T-junction, and immediately right into Jacob Street.
- At the T-junction, turn right into Mill Street.
- As Mill Street bends right, dismount and turn left to cross the mouth of St Saviour's Dock on the private footbridge.
- Remount to continue on the riverfront and turn left by the Design Museum into Maguire Street.
- Turn right at the T-junction onto Gainsford Street.
- Turn left at the crossroads onto Curlew Street to find the docking station.

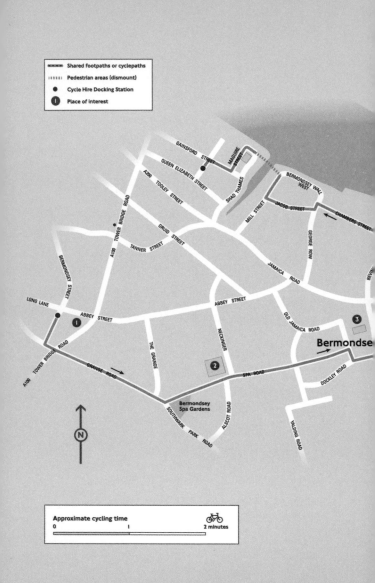

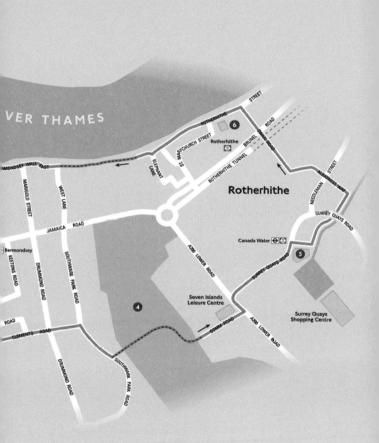

RIVER THAMES

MONDSEY WALL EAST

MARIGOLD STREET

WEST LANE

JAMAICA ROAD

Bermondsey

KEETONS ROAD

DRUMMOND ROAD

SOUTHWARK PARK ROAD

ROAD

CLEMENTS ROAD

DRUMMOND ROAD

SOUTHWARK PARK ROAD

ELEPHANT LANE

MAYCHURCH STREET

KING JS

ROTHERHITHE STREET

Rotherhithe

ROTHERHITHE TUNNEL

BRUNEL ROAD

Rotherhithe

Rotherhithe

SWANN ROAD

ALBATROSS WAY

NEEDLEMAN STREET

SURREY QUAYS ROAD

Canada Water

SURREY QUAYS ROAD

A200 LOWER ROAD

Seven Islands
Leisure Centre

SOMMA ROAD

A200 LOWER ROAD

Surrey Quays
Shopping Centre

6

5

4

BERMONDSEY SPA &
THE ROTHERHITHE COAST

PLACES OF INTEREST

❶ New Caledonian Market
Also known as the Bermondsey
Square Market, this antiques
market began life in Victorian
times just off the Caledonian
Road. It moved to its current
venue after the Second World
War when it reopened. Stalls are
set up at 5am on a Friday morning,
so you need to be an early riser
to catch a bargain.

❷ Old Bermondsey Town Hall
Originally built in 1881 and
now converted into apartments,
the town hall represents the
redevelopment of the area in the
late 19th and early 20th century
as river trade increased and the
railways arrived. Bermondsey
gained the nickname of 'Biscuit
Town' thanks to the company
Peek, Frean & Co., which was
based here until 1989.

❸ St James Church
Known as a Commissioners' or
Waterloo church, St James is one
of the churches built as an act of
national thanksgiving after the
defeat of Napoleon at Waterloo.

❹ Southwark Park
Renovated in 2001 thanks to the
Heritage Lottery Fund, the park
now has a new bowling pavilion
as well as a lake, a replica of the
original 1833 bandstand and
a children's play area. The park
also offers a café and art gallery,
sporting facilities and the Ada
Salter Rose Garden.

❺ Canada Water Library
This gleaming, stylish, Piers
Gough-designed library is shaped
like an inverted pyramid. A spiral
staircase leads from the entrance
and café on the ground-floor level
to the light, airy reading room
at the top of the building.

❻ Brunel Museum
Based in the Engine House built
by Sir Marc Brunel in 1842 for
the steam pumps that kept the
Thames Tunnel dry, this museum
tells the story of the Brunels'
work and how the tunnel was
constructed. The Grand Entrance
Hall was the world's first
underground theatre.

FROM THE OVAL TO BATTERSEA PARK

Flex those calf muscles as you head away from inner London via the historical sporting venue of The Oval towards the windy wastes of Clapham Common, and then enjoy rolling downhill – Lavender Hill, that is – as you make your way towards the amenities of Battersea Park.

DISTANCE 7km (4⅓ miles)
PROFILE Hills up and down
PICK UP DOCKING STATION Kennington Road Post Office, Oval
DROP OFF DOCKING STATION Prince of Wales Drive, Battersea Park

- Follow Bowling Green Street and turn right at the T-junction to go around Kennington Oval.
- At the T-junction, turn left to stay on Kennington Oval, and then use the light-controlled crossing to turn right onto the path into the estate.
- Turn right – to pass the docking station – on Meadow Road.
- At the T-junction turn left on Dorset Road, then right on Bolney Street; Bolney Street then becomes St Stephen's Terrace.
- Turn right at the T-junction onto Aldebert Terrace, then straight on at the traffic lights – over the South Lambeth Road into Thorne Road.
- Turn left onto Lansdowne Gardens and take the second exit from the roundabout to continue ahead on Lansdowne Gardens.
- At the crossroads go straight on into Larkhall Lane and cross the Give Way sign at the end of Jeffreys Road to continue on Larkhall Lane; Larkhall Lane goes uphill and becomes Larkhall Rise.
- Larkhall Rise becomes Rectory Grove, then Old Town.
- As you see green space ahead, bear right on Old Town, which becomes Clapham Common North Side. As the road becomes one way, cross to the left to continue on the contra-flow cycle path.

- Turn left away from the road on the path, then cross Clapham Common North Side using the light-controlled crossing. Turn right onto Clapham Common North Side and continue with the Common on your left.
- Go through the first set of traffic lights and, before the next, look behind, signal if necessary, and move to the right to go straight on, signposted 'Buses and Cycles Only'.
- Just before the docking station on the right, turn right into Marjorie Grove.
- At the T-junction turn right into Sisters Avenue.
- At the T-junction turn left into Thirsk Road.
- Go straight on over Lavender Hill and down Glycena Road.
- Bear right, and then at the T-junction turn left into Grayshott Road.
- At the T-junction turn right into Eversleigh Road.
- Just before the convenience store on the left, turn right into the unsigned cul-de-sac of Culvert Road.
- At the end turn right and walk up the ramp and over the footbridge.
- Go through the tunnel to continue on Culvert Road.
- At the T-junction turn right – physically straight on – to continue on Culvert Road passing The British Flag pub on your right.
- At the T-junction turn right onto Battersea Park Road.
- Turn left onto Beechmore Road.
- At the T-junction with Prince of Wales Drive, turn right to find the docking station on your left.

PLACES OF INTEREST

❶ The Oval

One of the legendary venues in cricketing history, the Oval has been the home of Surrey County Cricket Club since 1845. Over the years, it has clocked up a number of firsts in terms of events, including the first Test match to be held in England in 1880; the creation of the Ashes in 1882; the first International football match (between England and Scotland) in 1870; and the first FA Cup Final in 1872.

❷ Clapham Old Town

With a history stretching back to Roman times, Clapham has a fascinating past. Samuel Pepys spent the last two years of his life living in the Old Town, while the 18th–19th-century Clapham Sect was heavily involved in campaigns for social reform. The Old Town contains some fine examples of Georgian and Victorian homes, plus restaurants and cafés, as well as a leisure centre. Check out the Saturday Venn Street market and the Landor Theatre.

❸ Clapham Common

Originally part of the Manor of Clapham and now host to a number of festivals, the 89-ha (220-acre) common contains London's largest bandstand, ponds, tennis courts, playgrounds and a skateboard park. Many well-known figures have lived around the common, including the composer Edvard Grieg and the novelist Graham Greene.

❹ Battersea Park

With 81ha (200 acres) of space, this Grade II-listed Victorian park has much to offer visitors. Waterfowl, including heron and grebe, can be seen on the lake, while sports lovers are well served too. In the 1950s, the northern section of the park was developed as gardens as part of the Festival of Britain, and the park now features a water garden. Relax at the café, visit the zoo, or sit and enjoy the fountains.

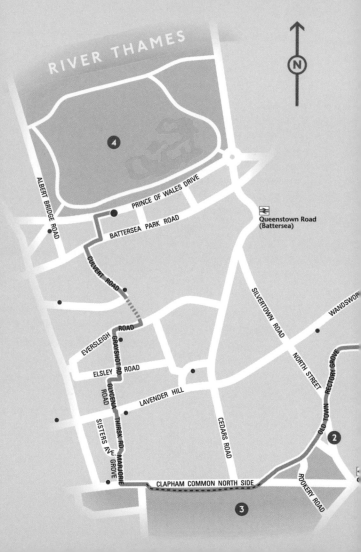

FROM THE OVAL
TO BATTERSEA PARK

N

RIVER THAMES

4

ALBERT BRIDGE ROAD

PRINCE OF WALES DRIVE

BATTERSEA PARK ROAD

Queenstown Road
(Battersea)

CULVERT ROAD

EVERSLEIGH ROAD

GRAYSHOTT RD

ELSLEY ROAD

GLYCENA ROAD

THIRSK RD

MARJORIE GROVE

SISTERS AVE.

LAVENDER HILL

SILVERTOWN ROAD

NORTH STREET

WANDSWOR

CEDARS ROAD

OLD TOWN

RECTORY GROVE

2

ROOKERY ROAD

CLAPHAM COMMON NORTH SIDE

3

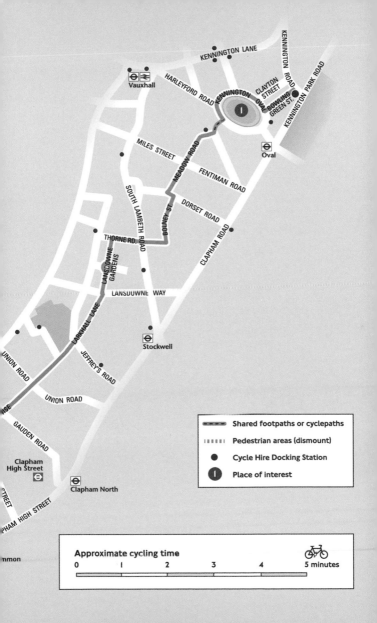

KENNINGTON LANE

HARLEYFORD ROAD

KENNINGTON ROAD

CLAYTON STREET

BOWLING GREEN ST.

KENNINGTON PARK ROAD

Vauxhall

KENNINGTON OVAL

Oval

MILES STREET

MEADOW ROAD

FENTIMAN ROAD

SOUTH LAMBETH ROAD

BOLNEY ST.

DORSET ROAD

THORNE RD.

CLAPHAM ROAD

LANSDOWNE GARDENS

LANSDOWNE WAY

LARKHALL LANE

Stockwell

UNION ROAD

JEFFREY'S ROAD

UNION ROAD

GAUDEN ROAD

Clapham High Street

Clapham North

CLAPHAM HIGH STREET

mmon

	Shared footpaths or cyclepaths
	Pedestrian areas (dismount)
●	Cycle Hire Docking Station
I	Place of interest

Approximate cycling time

0   1   2   3   4   5 minutes

THE RAILWAY
LANDS OF SURREY

Taking in the good, the bad and the ugly (architecturally speaking), this route is peppered with 19th-century terraces, but allows some respite in Burgess Park before you are enticed by the flavours of Brixton and some suggestions for sustenance.

DISTANCE 10km (6¼ miles), easily shortened to 8km (5 miles)
PROFILE Imperceptible climbing for a downhill finish
PICK UP DOCKING STATION Walworth Road, Southwark
DROP OFF DOCKING STATION Binfield Road, Stockwell

- Ride south-east – away from the Elephant and Castle roundabout – on the Walworth Road, passing under the railway bridge.
- Turn left onto Heygate Street.
- Continue on Rodney Road, then Flint Street.
- East Street – a turning to your right – has a street market everyday except Monday.
- Flint Street becomes Thurlow Street.
- At the traffic-light controlled T-junction, go straight on into Burgess Park.
- At the corner of the pond turn right and continue – keeping the square brick chimney of the baths and laundry to your left – to join Wells Way.
- The BMX track is ahead of you.
- Turn left on Wells Way.
- Turn right at the traffic-light controlled T-junction onto Southampton Way.
- Turn left through a modal filter at the next traffic lights by an orange brick wall onto a cycle path.
- Turn right onto Harris Street.

- At the T-junction, turn right on Edmund Street and immediately left onto Picton Street.
- At the T-junction by the British Queen pub, turn right into Brisbane Street, which becomes Caspian Street.
- Turn left onto New Church Road.
- Turn right just before the zebra crossing and left on the short cycle track to continue on New Church Road, and emerge on Camberwell Road with what was the Corrib Bar on your left.
- Turn left on Camberwell Road and right at the traffic lights into Wyndham Road.
- Go under the railway bridge, then left into Comber Grove.
- Turn right by the Hollington Youth Club into Redcar Street.
- Turn left into Councillor Street.
- Cross Camberwell New Road into Flodden Street.
- At the roundabout, take the first exit into Denmark Road, go under the railway bridge and turn right into Carew Street.
- Turn left on Lilford Road, then right onto Flaxman Road.
- At the crossroads, turn right onto Gordon Grove to repass under the railway.
- At the T-junction, turn left on Minet Street, then left again onto Loughborough Road.
- Turn right after the shops onto Barrington Road.
- Go under two parallel railway bridges and – at the traffic lights – turn right onto Coldharbour Lane; Southwyck House is on your left.
- At the next crossroads, pass under a railway bridge and turn right on Atlantic Road.
- Brixton Market is in the streets to your left every day except Sunday.
- At the light-controlled T-junction, turn right into Brixton Road.
- Take the first left into Ferndale Road and immediately right into the diagonal walking street leading to Stockwell Avenue. Continue ahead on Stockwell Avenue.
- At the T-junction, turn left into Stockwell Road. Stockwell Skatepark, also known as Brixton Beach, is to your right.

- Pass Brixton Cycles and the restaurant O Cantinho de Portugal on your right.
- Turn left into Stockwell Green. (If you are flagging, you can carry straight on along Stockwell Road to find the docking station to the right of Stockwell Underground Station.)
- At the T-junction, turn left into Landor Road; you will pass the Old Post Office Bakery on your left.
- At the junction by Clapham North Underground Station, you may have to dismount to cross through the plastic bollards and turn right on Bedford Road, then immediately turn right at the traffic lights onto Clapham Road, the Portsmouth Road and now Cycle Superhighway CS7.
- Run down CS7 to find the docking station in Binfield Road, just past Stockwell Underground Station on the left.

PLACES OF INTEREST

❶ East Street Market
Known locally as 'The Lane', this market is nowadays an excellent destination for African and Caribbean fruit and vegetables as well as household items, clothing, jewellery, CDs and DVDs. East Street was also the birthplace of Charlie Chaplin.

❷ Burgess Park
Southwark's largest park at 57ha (140 acres), it is also one of London's youngest parks, built between the 1950s and 1980s. It contains fascinating remnants of buildings, such as a lime kiln, and bridges that were used to cross the canal. In August, visitors can enjoy the Latin American Carnaval del Pueblo.

❸ Southwyck House
This development was intended as a barrier to deflect the sound of traffic on a flyover that was never built. Unsurprisingly, it became known as the Barrier Block. It was once the home of the artist Damien Hirst.

❹ Brixton Market
With around 80 stalls covering Electric Avenue, Pope's Road and Brixton Station Road, this is a lively market, with street music played on Thursday and Friday nights when there is late opening.

❺ Brixton Beach
Officially Stockwell Skatepark, but also known as 'Brixton Bowls', the park has been in use since it opened in 1978 and attracts BMX riders and rollerskaters as well as skateboarders.

❻ Brixton Cycles
For bikes and repairs, Brixton Cycles is the place. This workers' cooperative has been going strong for more than 30 years.

❼ O Cantinho de Portugal
Part deli, part restaurant, this popular place is dedicated to authentic Portuguese cuisine.

❽ The Old Post Office Bakery
Launched by a German teacher, Karl Heinz Rossbach, this bakery is famous for its sourdough.

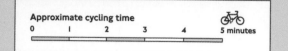

Approximate cycling time

| 0 | 1 | 2 | 3 | 4 | 5 minutes |

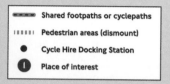

Shared footpaths or cyclepaths

Pedestrian areas (dismount)

Cycle Hire Docking Station

Place of interest

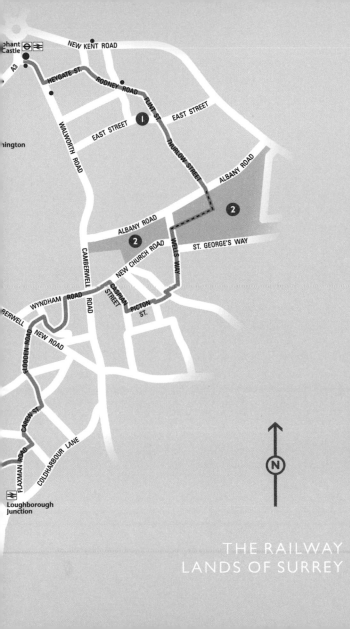

THE RAILWAY
LANDS OF SURREY

BATTERSEA VILLAGE TO MAN-MADE LAND & WATERSIDE CRANES

London's oldest village, Battersea, will throw up plenty to tempt, but carry on to appreciate the riverside St Mary's Church that attracted Turner to use it as a site for painting the Thames. Next head along to the park and the capital's biggest housing development and then on to enjoy some classic views of Westminster.

DISTANCE 8km (5 miles)

PROFILE Flat riverside riding, 1km (²/₃ mile) in the central section uses big roads that mostly have shared-use footpaths

PICK UP DOCKING STATION Albert Bridge Road, Battersea Park

DROP OFF DOCKING STATION Fire Brigade Pier, Vauxhall

- Walk north – against the one-way traffic flow on this section of Albert Bridge Road – towards the circus at the south-west corner of Battersea Park.
- Walk or ride across the junction to continue north on Albert Bridge Road, which is now two-way.
- There's a secluded docking station – Ethelburga Estate, Battersea Park – on the left by the zebra crossing, which can come in handy if you're riding circuits on Battersea Park.
- At the traffic lights, turn left onto Parkgate Road.
- Phoenix Cycles is on the left as you approach the traffic lights.
- At the traffic lights, go straight on into Westbridge Road. Pass the docking station.
- At the traffic lights, turn left on Vicarage Crescent through Battersea Square.

- As the river-frontage opens on your right you will see the Cremorne Railway Bridge.
- The road swings away from the Thames. Turn right before the Cremorne Railway Bridge – as if to enter Groveside Court – dismount and walk up the footpath to the bridge, and then turn right towards the river. When you reach the water, turn right to ride downstream.
- Most of the riverside paths in this ride are on private property where cycling is tolerated. Ride slowly near other people. Be polite. Don't put others in danger and don't make others feel endangered.
- If you're in a hurry, or want to ride fast, you can ride back to Battersea Park via the roads that brought you here.
- Continue with care, keeping close to the river, via St Mary's Churchyard.
- When you reach Albert Bridge, turn right away from the river and up the ramp to Albert Bridge Road.
- Cross the road and ride downhill away from the Bridge.
- Turn left into Battersea Park.
- Follow Carriage Drive North into the park. Pass the Peace Pagoda.
- After London Recumbents bicycle hire and the Pier Point Café, ignore the right turn signposted British Genius, and fork right away from the river, past the modal filter with the dark brown and white striped barrier pole, onto Carriage Drive East.
- At the T-junction turn left onto Carriage Drive South.
- (A right turn allows you to ride circuits of the park.)
- Exit the park through Rosary Gate.
- Take the second exit from the roundabout into Prince of Wales Drive; you can ride on the cycle path on the pavement or on the road.
- If you're using the path on the pavement, you will have to drop back onto the road to go under the railway bridge.
- At the traffic lights, turn left into Battersea Park Road. Pass Battersea Dogs & Cats Home on your left.
- After the Dogs & Cats Home the footpath becomes dual-use again, so you can ride on it if you wish.

- The building site on your left is the extensive Battersea Power Station redevelopment.
- As the river reappears on your left, ride carefully up onto the red-brick surface of William Henry Walk.
- Continue downstream; the notes above about riding on permitted paths also apply here.
- Go carefully under Vauxhall Bridge.
- Continue over the slipway – which is live with amphibious vehicle tourist-traffic – left by the bike sheds, and on downstream.
- At the Albert Embankment docking station, you have the choice to rejoin the road or continue politely on the pavement.
- You will find the next docking station – Fire Brigade Pier, Vauxhall – on the water-side of the road before Lambeth Bridge.

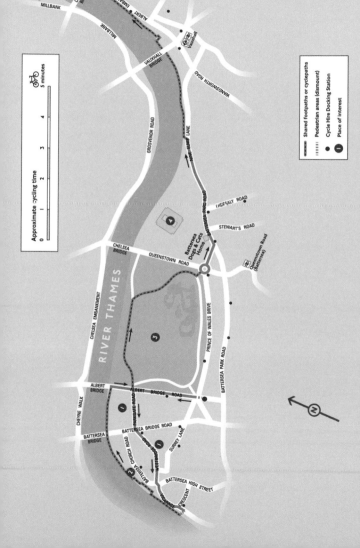

BATTERSEA VILLAGE
TO MAN-MADE LAND &
WATERSIDE CRANES

Approximate cycling time

0   1   2   3   4   5 minutes

Shared footpaths or cyclepaths

Pedestrian areas (dismount)

Cycle Hire Docking Station

Place of interest

RIVER THAMES

CHELSEA EMBANKMENT

MILLBANK

LAMBETH PALACE ROAD

LAMBETH BRIDGE

ALBERT EMBANKMENT

VAUXHALL BRIDGE

Vauxhall

WANDSWORTH ROAD

GROSVENOR ROAD

NINE ELMS LANE

THESSALY ROAD

STEWART'S ROAD

CHELSEA BRIDGE

QUEENSTOWN ROAD

Battersea Dogs & Cats Home

Queenstown Road (Battersea)

PRINCE OF WALES DRIVE

BATTERSEA PARK ROAD

ALBERT BRIDGE

ALBERT BRIDGE ROAD

CHEYNE WALK

BATTERSEA BRIDGE

BATTERSEA BRIDGE ROAD

SURREY LANE

PARKGATE ROAD

CHURCH ROAD

BATTERSEA HIGH STREET

CRESCENT

N

PLACES OF INTEREST

❶ Battersea Village
The origins of the village date back to the 7th century, making it the oldest village in London, and it is now probably best known as the site of the Battersea Dogs & Cats Home. The warehouses that sprang up during the Industrial Revolution are now luxury blocks of flats and the village is now packed with gastro pubs, delis, late-night bars and restaurants.

❷ St Mary's Church
Completed in 1777, this Georgian church is Grade II-listed. This is where the poet and artist William Blake was married and where British and American Army General Benedict Arnold is buried. Now the vestry was once used by the artist J.M.W. Turner as a viewpoint to paint the Thames.

❸ Battersea Park
(See page 71.)

❹ Battersea Power Station Development
Views of London from the south-west have long been dominated by the chimneys of the disused, Grade II-listed power station. Now in the throes of redevelopment after a long period of neglect, the refurbished site will include a mixture of offices and residences as well as shops and restaurants. A new park will be created on the riverside and a high street will link the railway station with a new tube station that will be created as part of a London Underground extension of the Northern Line to the area.

❺ Views of the Palace of Westminster
The south bank of the Thames offers some of the most recognisable views of the Palace of Westminster, whether reflected in the river during the day, or glowing with lights in the evening. It is well worth pausing to enjoy the true magnificence of Sir Charles Barry's design.

THE OLD EAST END

Enjoy a journey through Bethnal Green taking you from
Columbia Road and its renowned traditional flower market,
via the nostalgia of the V&A Museum of Childhood, to the
leafy delights of the Millennium Park, and along London's
oldest known trade route, to the spectacular Queen Elizabeth
II Olympic Park.

DISTANCE 5km (3 miles)

PROFILE No hills

PICK UP DOCKING STATION Columbia Road, Weavers

DROP OFF DOCKING STATION Wendon Street, Old Ford

- Ride east on Columbia Road.
- When the cobblestones begin, turn right onto Barnet Grove
  and immediately left onto Baxendale Street.
- At the T-junction, turn right on Durant Street and pass through
  the modal filter.
- Turn left at the crossroads on Gosset Street, which becomes
  Old Bethnal Green Road.
- Turn right at the T-junction on Cambridge Heath Road.
- Take the second left – at the traffic lights – onto Old Ford Road.
- Take the first right onto Victoria Park Square with the Museum
  of Childhood on your right.
- At the T-junction, turn left onto the Roman Road.
- After the traffic lights, turn right onto Bacton Street.
- Go round the gate and left at the crossroads onto Digby Street.
- Turn right at the crossroads onto Morpeth Street.
- Turn left at the crossroads onto Bullards Place.
- Cross Warley Street and go straight across and through the
  Gothic stone arch marked 'V.P.C. 1845' into Meath Gardens.
- On entering the park, turn then fork left to follow the paths carefully

- to exit Meath Gardens at their south-eastern corner with the railway tracks on your right and the curved block of flats on your left.
- Cross the Regents Canal on the new footbridge.
- The Palm Tree Pub is to your left. This is Millennium Park.
- As you reach the bottom of the ramp from the footbridge turn right in front of the metal gates on brick piers, then turn left to reach Grove Road.
- Cross Grove Road at the light-controlled crossing and pass the Victoria Pub into Arbery Road.
- Turn right on Medway Road and immediately left into Stanfield Road.
- Continue on the same line into Viking Close, Saxon Road and then turn right into Stafford Road.
- Turn left onto Tredegar Road.
- Turn left onto Parnell Road.
- Turn right onto Roman Road towards the giant red poppy sculptures. A right turn here takes you into Roman Road Market.
- At the Sculptures turn left onto Legion Terrace.
- At the T-junction turn right on Old Ford Road.
- The docking station here is currently at the edge of the zone, but you can go further to explore the Queen Elizabeth II Olympic Park, where there will soon be new docking stations.
- Go over the footbridge into Crown Close.
- At the roundabout take the first exit into Wick Lane.
- Turn right onto the Greenway to access the Olympic Park.

PLACES OF INTEREST

❶ Columbia Road
Best known for the flower market that takes place every Sunday starting at 8am, this Victorian road also has many great shops and cafés. The first market was established in 1869 and was a covered market selling food.

❷ V&A Museum of Childhood
Admire some delightful collections of clothes, toys, advertising and educational material from the last 300 years: one of the earliest rocking horses, an enchanting array of dolls' houses, and the complex products of the late 20th century.

❸ Meath Gardens
Named after the Earl of Meath, and originally a privately owned cemetery, the gardens were opened as a public space in 1894 and include a children's playground and a memorial to the Aboriginal cricketer, King Cole.

❹ Millennium Park
Forming part of Mile End Park, this section opened in 2004 after a £25 million refurbishment that saw the construction of a Piers Gough-designed bridge which links the park with the other side of the Mile End Road.

❺ Palm Tree Pub
Ideal for jazz lovers, the Palm Tree is a welcoming pub where you can sit outside in summer.

❻ Roman Road Market
Standing on the oldest trade route in the UK, stalls sell everything from bric-a-brac to food and books; adjacent markets specialise in arts and crafts (Saturdays) and local produce (first Saturday each month).

❼ Queen Elizabeth II Olympic Park
Dominated by the UK's largest piece of public art, the ArcelorMittal Orbit, the park is still home to at least four sports venues, but now boasts four interactive trails that meander through 227ha (560 acres) of parkland, and is set to become a new centre of the arts.

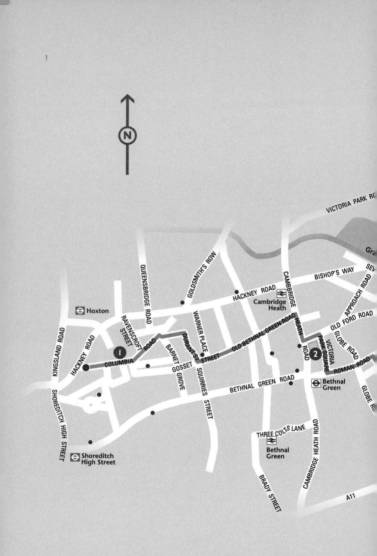

THE OLD EAST END

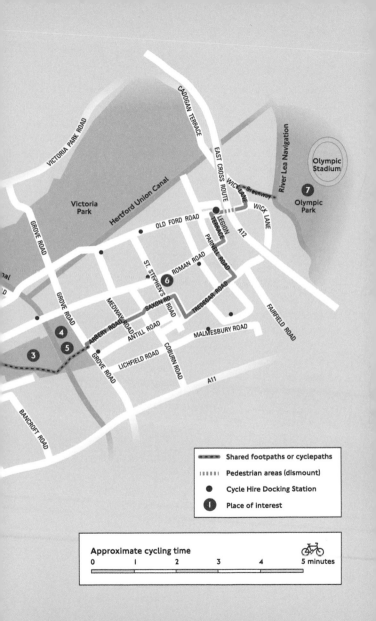

VICTORIA PARK ROAD

CADOGAN TERRACE

EAST CROSS ROUTE

WICK LANE

Greenway

River Lea Navigation

Olympic
Stadium

Victoria
Park

Hertford Union Canal

Olympic
Park

7

GROVE ROAD

OLD FORD ROAD

LEGION TERRACE

PARNELL ROAD

A12

WICK LANE

ST. STEPHEN'S RD.

ROMAN ROAD

6

GROVE ROAD

MEDWAY ROAD

SAXON RD.

ARBERY ROAD

ANTILL ROAD

TREDEGAR ROAD

FAIRFIELD ROAD

4

5

3

GROVE ROAD

LICHFIELD ROAD

COBURN ROAD

MALMESBURY ROAD

A11

BANCROFT ROAD

Shared footpaths or cyclepaths

Pedestrian areas (dismount)

● Cycle Hire Docking Station

1 Place of interest

Approximate cycling time

0   1   2   3   4   5 minutes

TOWER TO TOWER

Travelling east along the Thames, this route moves from the Bloody Tower to the new towers of West India Docks on the Isle of Dogs, taking in many areas that would have been familiar to the sailors and merchants of the 18th and 19th centuries, when Britain was at the height of its seafaring power.

DISTANCE 6km (3¾ miles)
PROFILE No hills
PICK UP DOCKING STATION Tower Gardens (Tower Hill)
DROP OFF DOCKING STATION Fisherman's Walk West (Canary Wharf)

- Ride west (left) on Tower Hill.
- First left – between yellow stone blocks – onto the pedestrian area of Petty Wales.
- Dismount at the gates by the Tower of London gift shop and walk down towards the river with the Middle Tower on your left.
- Turn left onto The Wharf and walk past Traitors' Gate to pass under the northernmost arch of Tower Bridge. Once through the gate you may remount.
- Bear left in front of the Starbucks coffee shop, then right onto the covered hotel access road onto St Katharine's Way.
- Cross the metal bascule bridge. You may choose to walk as the advisory sign suggests.
- Pass the St Katharine's Way docking station. When the paths around the Tower are very busy, you may choose to walk the first section and pick up a bike here.
- Turn right at the T-junction onto Wapping High Street.
- Shortly turn left into Redmead Lane; keep left to run along the right side of the ornamental basin.
- Go down the hairpin ramps to the right of the steps and along the left bank of the ornamental canal, signposted 'Shadwell Basin'.

- Bear left when the canal divides.
- Bear right when the canal bends.
- Bear left through Wapping Woods.
- Bear right to follow another length of ornamental canal under a red metal bascule bridge to reach Shadwell Basin.
- Double back to go round the north (left) side of Shadwell Basin, passing the high wall of St Paul's Church, Shadwell.
- At Glamis Road, turn right to cross the red metal bridge if you want to visit The Wapping Project or the Prospect of Whitby pub.
- The route proper continues with a left and right onto a path beside the park, signposted 'Thames Path'.
- Turn left off Thames Path just before the steps onto the wooden bridge.
- Turn right, then left through brick housing estate to reach The Highway.
- Turn right along the dual-use footpath towards the Limehouse Link Tunnel entrance.
- Turn right into Narrow Street.
- Continue on Narrow Street; the road is one-way for motor-traffic but two-way for bikes, so you will be riding against the motor-traffic flow.
- Continue on Narrow Street to pass The Narrow restaurant and bar, and cross the bridge over the entry lock of the Limehouse Basin.
- Narrow Street becomes Limehouse Causeway.
- Turn right onto Salter Street before the road goes under the Docklands Light Railway (DLR).
- Bear left onto the blue stripe across the footpath in front of Westferry DLR station. Cross Westferry Road on the light-controlled crossing.
- Turn left – by the Salvation Army – on to the dual-use footpath.
- Turn right towards Cineworld cinema, then right into Hertsmere Road by the Museum of London Docklands.
- Turn left at the mini-roundabout, opposite Ontario Way, into the car park.
- Carefully turn right around the blind corner to follow the edge of the Middle Dock to the Fisherman's Walk Docking Station.

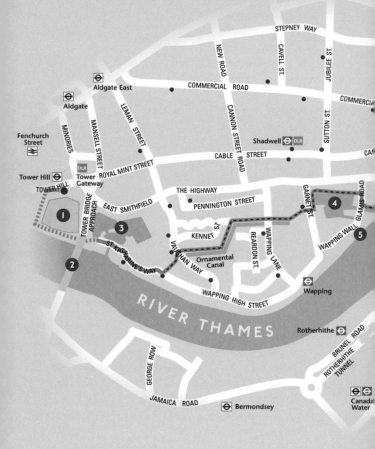

TOWER TO TOWER

STEPNEY WAY

NEW ROAD

CAVELL ST.

JUBILEE ST.

COMMERCIAL ROAD

COMMERCIAL

Aldgate East

Aldgate

LEMAN STREET

MANSELL STREET

CANNON STREET ROAD

SUTTON ST.

CA

Shadwell ⊖ DLR

Fenchurch Street

MINORIES

CABLE STREET

Tower Hill ⊖

DLR
Tower Gateway

ROYAL MINT STREET

THE HIGHWAY

GARNET ST.

GLAMIS ROAD

TOWER HILL

EAST SMITHFIELD

PENNINGTON STREET

4

1

TOWER BRIDGE APPROACH

3

KENNET ST.

WAPPING WALL

5

VAUGHAN WAY

REARDON ST.

WAPPING LANE

2

ST. KATHARINE'S WAY

Ornamental Canal

⊖ Wapping

WAPPING HIGH STREET

RIVER THAMES

Rotherhithe ⊖

BRUNEL ROAD

ROTHERHITHE TUNNEL

GEORGE ROW

JAMAICA ROAD

⊖ Bermondsey

⊖⊖
Canada Water

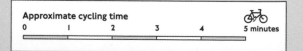

Approximate cycling time

0   1   2   3   4   🚲 5 minutes

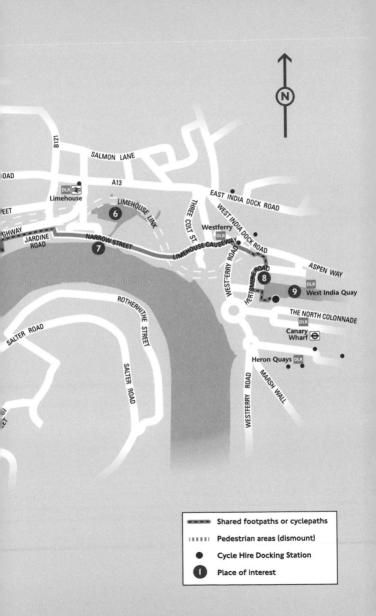

PLACES OF INTEREST

❶ Tower of London

The Tower has been at the heart of British history since the reign of William the Conqueror. Associated with many historical figures, and home to the Crown Jewels, it is has had many functions, including that of a zoo. Henry III once kept a polar bear here. Presented to him in 1251, it was allowed an extra long chain so that it could go and fish in the Thames. In 2014, the Tower attracted record crowds to see Paul Cummins' and Tom Piper's installation, *Blood Swept Lands and Seas of Red*, which covered the moat in a sea of red ceramic poppies to commemorate the British Forces' dead of the First World War.

❷ Tower Bridge

For many, this famous Victorian bridge is synonymous with London, with its towers that support a double walkway, now fitted with a glass floor, and a suspension bridge across the Thames. Consisting of more than 11,000 tonnes of steel, the bridge offers amazing panoramic views of London and even acts as a wedding venue.

❸ St Katharine's Dock

Now a thriving marina and an office, dining and retail site, St Katharine's Dock was once a major centre of maritime commerce, heady with the aroma of spices, tobacco, rum and tea. Its history is still apparent in the renovated warehouses that were originally designed by the engineer Thomas Telford and the architect Philip Hardwick.

❹ Shadwell Basin

Like many London docks, by the end of the 19th century, Shadwell proved too small to accommodate the ever-increasing size of cargo ships, and it closed to shipping in 1969. The former home of Captain James Cook and the birthplace of Thomas Jefferson, it is now a bustling residential area that offers great facilities to keen sailors, canoeists and fishermen.

❺ The Prospect of Whitby
This is the site of London's oldest riverside tavern, with a history that stretches back to 1520, though not much remains of the original building. But if ghosts could talk, there would be plenty of tales of smugglers and footpads, as well as great artistic and literary figures, such as J.M.W. Turner and Samuel Pepys.

❻ Limehouse Basin
An excellent mooring for canal and river boats, the Basin forms a link between the Thames and the Regent's Canal. Paths along the canal offer yet further routes for cycling or walking. Nearby Narrow Street houses The Grapes, a pub that features in Charles Dickens' *Our Mutual Friend* and is now leased by the actor Sir Ian McKellen.

❼ The Narrow Restaurant
Owned by Gordon Ramsay, this riverside gastro pub was once a dockmaster's house. The patio offers excellent views of the Thames in both directions.

❽ Museum of London, Docklands
Specialising in the history of the Thames and the Docklands, the museum houses the collection and archives of the Port of London Authority. With excellent exhibits for children, the galleries are arranged chronologically, beginning in Roman times and moving through to the present day.

❾ West India Docks
Part of the Canary Wharf rebuilding programme, the Docks were originally one of the most ambitious public works undertaken at the beginning of the 19th century. They had an innovative arrangement that allowed ships to enter the Import dock and unload and then sail round to the Export dock and take new cargo on board.

NEW HACKNEY

This ride takes you from the amenities of Shoreditch Park to the vibrant Hoxton Market and on to a game of cricket on London Fields. Or if that's not your thing, move on to sample the wares in Well Street, enjoy a roam around Victoria Park and then pick up some great food in Broadway Market.

DISTANCE 9km (5½ miles)
PROFILE Almost flat with a little gentle up and down north of Victoria Park
PICK UP DOCKING STATION Leonard Circus, Shoreditch
DROP OFF DOCKING STATION Regent's Row, Haggerston

- From the docking station, ride east towards the big round sculpture and turn left onto Paul Street.
- At the top of Paul Street, follow the cycle track across the footpath; Pitfield Street is ahead. Use the two light-controlled crossings – on Great Eastern Street, then Old Street – to get to it.
- Continue up Pitfield Street. At the roundabout, take the third exit to continue up Pitfield Street, with St John's Church, Hoxton on your left.
- At the corner of Shoreditch Park, turn right into Ivy Street. (If you want to relax in the park, there's a docking station in Bridport Place.)
- Emerge from the alley in Hoxton Street with care. (There is a street market here every day except Sunday.)
- Turn left on Hoxton Street, then right into Nuttall Street.
- Cross the Kingsland Road at the traffic lights to continue straight on along Whiston Road.
- Turn left into Swimmers Lane just before Haggerston Baths.
- Turn left on Laburnham Street and immediately right – by the Bridge Academy – to cross the Regent's Canal on Haggerston Road.
- After All Saints Church – opposite Stonebridge Gardens – turn right through the modal filter into Albion Drive.

- Go straight on at Queensbridge Road.
- At the T-junction with Lansdowne Drive, turn left and then right, to enter London Fields on the cycle path; the Lido is on your left.
- Cross the park and exit turning left on Martello Street.
- Pass the Pub on the Park, go under the bridge, and cross Richmond Road onto the cycle track.
- At Reading Lane turn right, then left, onto Mare Street.
- Go ahead past Hackney Town Hall and the Hackney Empire, and as the road bends left under the railway bridge, turn right – straight on – into Mare Street Narrow Way.
- Turn right carefully across the footpath to pass the Old Tower and climb gently into the churchyard.
- At the cross-path turn right; if you come to Sutton Place, you've gone too far.
- Turn left on Morning Lane. If the traffic lights are red, wait in the right lane to continue on Morning Lane.
- Well Street is on the right; the market is every day except Sunday.
- Continue straight on into Kenton Road.
- At the traffic lights on Cassland Road, go straight on into Gascoyne Road with Well Street Common on your right.
- At the T-junction with Harrowgate Road, turn right and then immediately cross Victoria Park Road and enter Victoria Park (the park closes at dusk), with the People's Park Tavern on your left.
- Turn right and follow the roadway along the Park Perimeter. Exit the park gates, cross Grove Road and re-enter the park on the other side.
- Turn left and ride around the ornamental lake; the lake is on your right.
- As you bear right, the Regent's Canal borders the park behind the railings to your left.
- Cross the fenced roadway and continue in the park parallel to the canal.
- When the roadway bears right, turn left to find the canal path and turn right. Ride slowly and be polite if the path is busy.
- Continue to Broadway Market and exit the canal path to the right just before the Lock to find the docking station in Regent's Row.

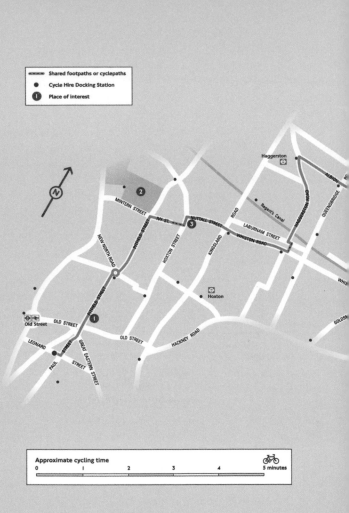

Shared footpaths or cyclepaths

● **Cycle Hire Docking Station**

❶ **Place of interest**

Haggerston

Regent's Canal

MINTERN STREET

NEW NORTH ROAD

SHEFFIELD STREET

IVY ST.

HOXTON STREET

NUTTALL STREET

KINGSLAND

ROAD

LABURNAM STREET

WHISTON ROAD

ALBION

QUEENSBRIDGE

Hoxton

Old Street

LEONARD

PAUL STREET

SHEFFIELD STREET

GREAT EASTERN STREET

OLD STREET

OLD STREET

HACKNEY ROAD

GOLDSM

WHIST

Approximate cycling time

0   1   2   3   4   5 minutes

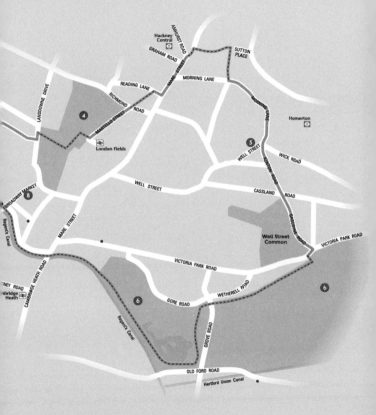

PLACES OF INTEREST

❶ CycleLab & Juice Bar, Pitfield Street

Enjoy a veggie or fruit smoothie while you wait for your bike to be repaired in this friendly shop-cum-juice bar. Knowledgeable staff will answer any bike-related queries and set your bike back on the road in great condition.

❷ Shoreditch Park

This Green Flag-award winner was once covered in terraces, but the bombs of the Second World War destroyed much of the housing and after a period of temporary pre-fab, the area was made into a park in the early 1970s. Covering 7.7ha (19 acres), it offers many amenities such as a beach volleyball court, football and rugby pitches, tennis courts, play areas and an amphitheatre.

❸ Hoxton Street Market

Now a very fashionable area, the first record of Hoxton is in the Domesday Book, when it was listed as 'Hoggesdon'. Selling a mixture of food, household items and clothes, this laid-back market is ideal for bargain hunting. Check out the renowned White Cube Gallery in nearby Hoxton Square and, if you fancy training as a clown, try the National Centre for Circus Arts in the former Shoreditch Electric Light Station.

❹ London Fields

First recorded in 1540, this former piece of common land was used by drovers to rest livestock that they were taking to market in London. Nowadays, it is cricket lovers who head here because the North East London Cricket League looks upon the fields as its principal home. In fact, a game of cricket was first played here in 1802. With a market selling a variety of different products on Saturdays and thriving farmers' market on every Sunday at the primary school, plus tennis courts, a BMX track, a lido and children's play areas, there is something for everyone.

❺ Well Street Market

Back in the mid-15th century, this was a well-to-do area with moated pilgrim houses on either side, and by the 19th century Well Street was a prosperous shopping area, known for its leather works. The market has been in existence since the 1850s, and it was here that Jack Cohen, the founder of Tesco supermarkets, began his career in sales by working as a barrow boy. The area now attracts numerous artists as represented by Karin Janssen's Project Space Gallery at 213 Well Street. Former famous residents of Well Street include the traveller Celia Fiennes, who has a building named after on the corner of Well Street and Mare Street.

⑥ Victoria Park
(See page 47.)

⑦ Lock 7, Pritchard's Row
Opened in 2008, Lock 7 was actually the first cycle café in London. It's a great spot for relaxing by the canal, and customers can sit and enjoy a meal or snack while experts in the cycle shop work on their machines.

⑤ Broadway Market
Established as a market site in the 1890s, when you would have heard the sound of barrow boys touting their wares, Broadway started out as a fruit and vegetable market. Nowadays, more than 100 stalls still offer fresh food, a lot of it organic, but also a variety of other goods. The market is also surrounded by a plentiful array of tempting shops, restaurants and cafés. Look for vintage clothing or head for a plate of jellied eels, or just take home some fresh bread and delicious cheese.

AMONG THE
SQUARE LAGOONS

More water than land, this route through the Isle of Dogs,
which once housed King Henry VIII's hunting hounds, is
a journey through an area that was vital to the country's
overseas trade, but which now mixes business with pleasure.

DISTANCE 4km (2½ miles)

PROFILE No hills

PICK UP DOCKING STATION Upper Bank Street, Canary Wharf

DROP OFF DOCKING STATION Saunders Ness Road, Cubitt Town

- Ride south (right) on Upper Bank Street.
- Follow the square around, then turn left onto Bank Street under the DLR.
- Turn left at the traffic lights onto Marsh Wall. Turn right across the dual-use footpath in front of South Quay DLR Station to go south, passing Tompkins Attic Bar on your right with Millwall Inner Dock on your left.
- Pass Byblos Harbour, Lebanese restaurant, on your right.
- At the end of the dock, turn left on Pepper Street over Glengall Bridge.
- Turn right, pass the Manjal Restaurant on your left and the Outer Dock on your right.
- Turn left onto the curving path – before the tall brick chimney – pass under the DLR, then climb the hairpin path up to East Ferry Road.
- Turn right on East Ferry Road; the entrance to Mudchute Park is straight ahead.
- Go left onto the footpath at the zebra crossing and walk down the ramp into Millwall Park. Bear right around the park.
- Emerge from the park by Island Gardens DLR Station.
- Cross Manchester Road and ride carefully up Douglas Path.
- Turn Left on Saunders Ness Road to find the docking station; Island Gardens and the foot tunnel for Greenwich are straight ahead.

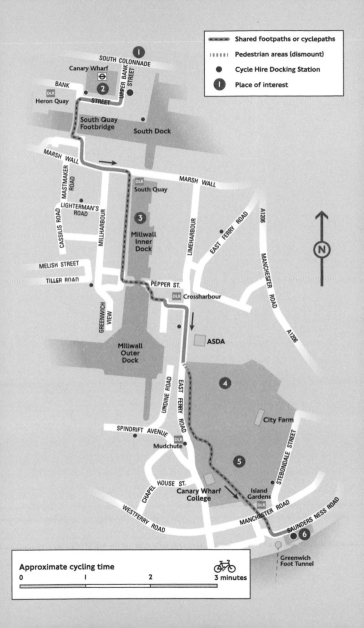

Legend

- ━ ━ Shared footpaths or cyclepaths
- ┊┊┊┊ Pedestrian areas (dismount)
- ● Cycle Hire Docking Station
- ❶ Place of interest

SOUTH COLONNADE

Canary Wharf

BANK
Heron Quay
STREET

UPPER BANK STREET

South Quay
Footbridge
South Dock

MARSH WALL

MASTMAKER ROAD
LIGHTERMAN'S ROAD
CASSILIS ROAD
MILLHARBOUR

South Quay

MARSH WALL

LIMEHARBOUR

EAST FERRY ROAD

A1206

MANCHESTER ROAD

Millwall Inner Dock

MELISH STREET
TILLER ROAD

GREENWICH VIEW

PEPPER ST.

Crossharbour

Millwall Outer Dock

UNDINE ROAD

EAST FERRY ROAD

ASDA

City Farm

SPINDRIFT AVENUE

Mudchute

STEBONDALE STREET

CHAPEL HOUSE ST.

Canary Wharf College

Island Gardens

WESTFERRY ROAD

MANCHESTER ROAD

SAUNDERS NESS ROAD

Greenwich Foot Tunnel

N

Approximate cycling time

0 — 1 — 2 — 3 minutes

PLACES OF INTEREST

❶ Canary Wharf

One of London's two main financial centres, Canary Wharf covers part of the old West India Docks. It now contains approximately 1,301,000 sq. m (14,000,000 sq. ft) of office and retail space and One Canada Square, which lies at its heart, is the UK's second tallest building.

❷ Jubilee Park

An oasis of calm among the buildings of Canary Wharf, Jubilee Park is in reality a rooftop garden, lying over the Jubilee Line Tube station. Running through the park is a serpentine water channel and the area contains numerous trees that provide colour and shade throughout the year.

❸ Millwall Docks

Home to the Docklands Sailing and Watersports centre, Millwall Docks was originally created in the 1860s to provide wharves for shipbuilding and repairwork. In 1999, the dock was used as a location in a James Bond film, *The World is Not Enough*, and in 2013 it was the venue for the Great London Swim.

❹ Mudchute Park and City Farm

This 13-ha (32-acre) oasis is home to one of the largest inner-city farms in Europe. With more than 100 animals representing many rare British breeds, it's a must-see for children, and offers invaluable educational services to local schools.

❺ Millwall Park

Popular with joggers, this small park offers plenty of facilities for playing football and rugby. Signs of its former use as part of the dockland industry can be seen in the disused railway viaduct.

❻ Island Gardens

Standing at the northern entrance to the Greenwich Foot Tunnel, the gardens offer amazing views across the Thames of the Cutty Sark and the old Royal Naval College, which is part of the Maritime Greenwich World Heritage site.

FROM VENICE TO HOLLAND

Potter along the towpaths around Paddington Basin and
Little Venice before heading for a spot of shopping in trendy
Portobello Road Market and a respite in Holland Park. With
buzzing restaurants, beautifully decorated narrowboats
and a little bit of opera at the end, there's a lot on offer.

DISTANCE 7km (4⅓ miles)
PROFILE Mostly downhill with some climbing near the end.
The last – very steep – hill, and the gentle downhill finish, can
be walked if you drop your bike off early
PICK UP DOCKING STATION North Wharf Road, Paddington
DROP OFF DOCKING STATION Holland Park, Kensington or
Lansdowne Road, Ladbroke Grove

- Cross Paddington Basin using the footbridge behind the docking
  station and turn right to follow the towpath west. Take care if the
  path is busy and don't hurry.
- Follow the towpath to and beside Browning's Pool, with three
  entrances.
- At the first exit to the pool, keep left up the ramp to emerge by
  the Canal Theatre. Go straight on into Delamere Terrace.
- When the road bends left away from the canal, go straight on –
  through the black semi-barriers – onto the dual-use path through
  the small park with St Mary Magdalene Church on your left.
- Rejoin the canal towpath.
- At the concrete footbridge with the spiral ramps, turn left onto
  Wedlake Street to emerge on Kensal Road.
- Turn left and continue to Trellick Tower, where the road bends right
  and becomes Golborne Road.

- At the mini-roundabout take the second exit – onto the metal railway bridge – to stay on Golborne Road.
- Portobello Road – with a market every day except Sunday and Thursday afternoons – is on your left.
- Take the next left – after Portobello Road – onto St Lawrence Terrace.
- Turn right onto Oxford Gardens and cross Ladbroke Grove at the traffic lights.
- At the mini-roundabout take the first exit into St Marks Road.
- Continue under the flyover with the docking station on your left.
- At the mini-roundabout take the third exit – to turn right – into Cornwall Crescent.
- At the T-junction, turn left to pass the docking station on Clarendon Road.
- Turn right into Portland Road and follow it round to the left.
- Bear right, then left to stay on Portland Road.
- Where the road is blocked, turn right onto Hippodrome Place.
- Where the road bends right, turn left – through the modal filter – then turn left to go into Pottery Lane with St Francis of Assisi Church on your left, and the what used to be the Earl of Zetland pub on your right.
- Follow Pottery Lane to rejoin Portland Road and turn right.
- At the traffic lights, turn left on Holland Park Avenue.
- (If you don't want to ride up a steep hill, you can drop your bike at the station on the left in Lansdowne Road.)
- Turn right into the first road on the right, Holland Park, then stop on the left and continue on foot up the south side of Holland Park Avenue. (You may prefer to continue to the junction with Ladbroke Grove and cross Holland Park Avenue using the traffic lights.)
- You will find the discreet entrance to Holland Walk a few metres east (uphill) of the junction of Holland Park and Holland Park Avenue.
- Engage bottom gear and ride up the dual-use path.
- Cross the summit and roll gently down to the docking station by the park entrance.

PLACES OF INTEREST

❶ Paddington Basin

This basin formed the junction of the Regent's and Grand Junction Canals. Since 2000, the area has undergone extensive redevelopment as part of the Paddington Waterside scheme, which includes a mixture of office and housing and two unusual bridges: the Rolling Bridge and the Fan Bridge.

❷ Little Venice

The origins of the name 'Little Venice' are disputed: some say that it was coined by the poet Robert Browning, others that it was Lord Byron. Apart from the beautifully painted narrowboats, you can enjoy cafés, restaurants, a floating art gallery and a puppet theatre. Try a trip on the waterbus service that operates from Little Venice and heads east to London Zoo and Camden Town.

❸ Trellick Tower

Designed in the Brutalist style by the Hungarian architect and furniture designer Ernö Goldfinger, this 31-storey block of flats is a Grade II-listed building, where a number of young designers are developing studios and outlets. It has also been used as a location for numerous films and music videos.

❹ Portobello Road Market

Once known as Green Lane, Portobello Road first hosted a fresh food market in the mid-19th century, but by the end of the Second World War, rag and bone men had begun to sell second-hand items and antiques. Many young designers have started out by having stalls here.

❺ Holland Park

This peaceful park was once the grounds of Holland House, which was owned by the 6th Earl of Ilchester and is now a ruin. In recent years, the ruins have been used as the backdrop for the open air Holland Park Theatre. With an ecology centre, orangery, cricket pitch, tennis courts and a giant chess set, there is a lot to do.

FROM VENICE
TO HOLLAND

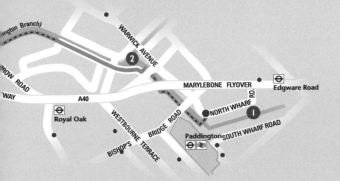

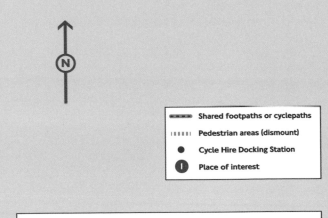

Shared footpaths or cyclepaths

Pedestrian areas (dismount)

Cycle Hire Docking Station

Place of interest

Approximate cycling time

| 0 | 1 | 2 | 3 | 4 | 5 minutes |

ROUND THE BEND

Venture to the west with a trip that will take you round the curving lowlands of Hammersmith and Chelsea – from the Victorian splendour of Hammersmith Bridge via award-winning cuisine to an Episcopal summer retreat and fun in the park.

DISTANCE 8km (5 miles) round trip
PROFILE Flat and easy
PICK UP DOCKING STATION Bridge Avenue, Hammersmith
DROP OFF DOCKING STATION as above

- Go south on Bridge Avenue, away from King's Street, towards Great West Road.
- Use the light-controlled crossings to go under the flyover into Bridge View.
- At the end of Bridge View, turn left to reach Hammersmith Bridge Road.
- Turn right on Hammersmith Bridge Road; before the bridge dismount and divert down the alley to the left to the river path and turn left.
- Turn left, away from the river, then right into Crisp Road parallel to the river.
- Turn right on the narrow path just past the Riverside Studios to take you back to the river.
- Turn left and continue along the Thames Path.
- After the path turns left, turn right onto Rainville Road.
- After The Crabtree pub, turn right down another small alley back to the river.
- After the path turns left, turn right onto Stevenage Road.
- After Craven Cottage (Fulham Football Club), go through the gates on the right into Bishop's Park, back towards the river.
- Follow the edge of the park to exit onto Putney Bridge Approach.

- Turn right, go over Putney Bridge and then – as you leave the bridge – turn right into Lower Richmond Road, and right to rejoin the path beside the river heading west.
- Follow the path by the river to Hammersmith Bridge.
- Immediately before the bridge, turn left to join the road and right to cross Hammersmith Bridge.
- Turn left to retrace your route to the docking station.

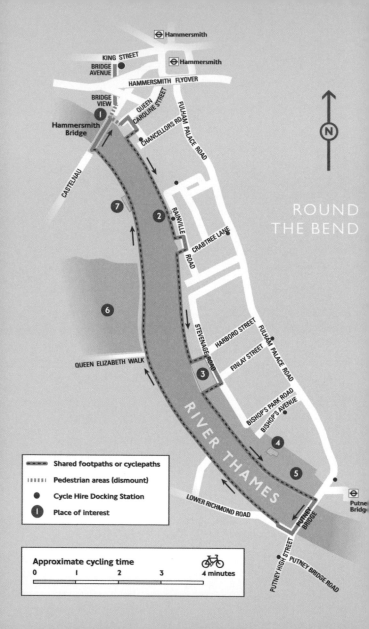

ROUND THE BEND

PLACES OF INTEREST

❶ Hammersmith Bridge
This Grade II-listed suspension bridge was designed by Sir Joseph Bazalgette. The bridge is decorated with the coats of arms of the UK, the Cities of London, Westminster, Colchester and Guildford and the counties of Kent and Middlesex.

❷ The River Café
This riverside Italian restaurant was opened in 1987 by Ruth Rogers and the late Rose Gray. Among the chefs who have worked here in the past are Jamie Oliver, Hugh Fearnley-Whittingstall and Theo Randall.

❸ Craven Cottage
Home to Fulham Football Club since 1896, the main stand and the corner pavilion are both Grade II-listed structures. With a capacity of 25,700, the ground is named after a royal hunting lodge that once stood on the site.

❹ Fulham Palace
For more than 12 centuries, there has been a bishop's residence here. It was formerly the country home of the Bishop of London, and now visitors can dine in the Drawing Room restaurant and enjoy the landscaped grounds.

❺ Bishop's Park
This Grade II-listed park contains an urban beach, children's playgrounds, bowling green and various other sports facilities as well as various landscape features. It was once part of the land of the nearby Fulham Palace.

❻ London Wetland Centre
Run by the Wildfowl & Wetlands Trust, this award-winning centre is home to hundreds of birds, animals, insects and bats. Children can enjoy the Discovery Centre and adventure playground.

❼ Harrods Furniture Depository
Now known as 'Harrods Village', the depository held large items of furniture for the department store in Knightsbridge. A well-known marker on the route of the Oxford and Cambridge Boat Race, these former warehouses are Grade II listed.

ALBERTOPOLIS

Marvel at the fulfilment of Prince Albert's 19th-century dream of a cultural centre, as you travel around what was once an agricultural heartland, and which now contains some of the greatest centres of scientific, artistic and historical importance in the capital.

DISTANCE 7km (4⅓ miles)
PROFILE Gentle climbing from the Thames almost to Hyde Park
PICK UP DOCKING STATION Eccleston Place, Victoria
DROP OFF DOCKING STATION Sedding Street, Sloane Square

- From the docking station, walk the short distance east – against the one-way flow to Eccleston Street – and turn left.
- Turn left onto the contra-flow cycle lane in Ebury Street.
- Turn right at the T-junction onto Pimlico Road.
- Go straight on at the traffic lights on Chelsea Bridge Road into Royal Hospital Road.
- Outside the Chelsea Physic Garden, turn right into Christchurch Street.
- At the church turn left across the modal filter into Robinson Street.
- At the crossroads go straight on over Flood Street into St Loo Avenue.
- Turn right onto Chelsea Manor Street.
- Cross the King's Road and continue on Chelsea Manor Street.
- At the T-junction turn left onto Britten Street. Then right onto Sydney Street.
- Turn left onto Cale Street.
- Turn right onto Dovehouse Street, then left onto South Parade.
- At the T-junction turn right, cross the Fulham Road at the traffic lights into Selwood Terrace, which becomes Onslow Gardens.
- Go straight on at the traffic lights into Queen's Gate.
- Climb Queen's Gate and turn right into Prince Consort Road. (If you carry on to the top, you come to Hyde Park.)

- Turn right into Exhibition Road.
- At the traffic lights go straight ahead to stay on Exhibition Road, then bear right into Thurloe Place.
- Pass South Kensington Tube Station, turn left, and left again, into Pelham Street.
- At the traffic lights by the Michelin Building on the Fulham Road, turn left and immediately right into Draycott Avenue.
- As Draycott Avenue becomes one-way, against you, bear left into Walton Street.
- Turn right into Beauchamp Place, which becomes Pont Street.
- Cross Sloane Street at the traffic lights, then turn right into Cadogan Place to run south, with Cadogan Place Gardens to your right.
- At the T-junction, turn left to stay on Cadogan Place and bear right into D'Oyley Street.
- Bear right into Sloane Terrace, then turn left to find the docking station in Sedding Street.

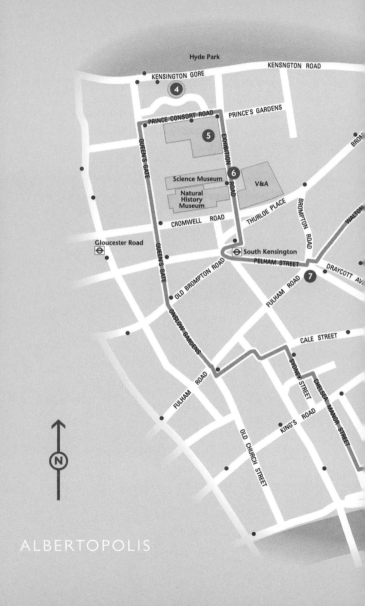

ALBERTOPOLIS

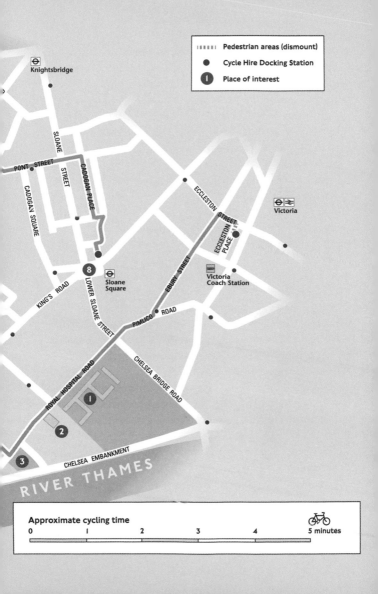

Pedestrian areas (dismount)

● **Cycle Hire Docking Station**

❶ **Place of interest**

Knightsbridge

SLOANE STREET

PONT STREET

CADOGAN PLACE

CADOGAN SQUARE

ECCLESTON STREET

Victoria

ECCLESTON PLACE

❽

Sloane
Square

KING'S ROAD

LOWER SLOANE STREET

EBURY STREET

Victoria
Coach Station

PIMLICO ROAD

ROYAL HOSPITAL ROAD

CHELSEA BRIDGE ROAD

❶

❷

❸

CHELSEA EMBANKMENT

RIVER THAMES

Approximate cycling time

| 0 | 1 | 2 | 3 | 4 | 5 minutes |

PLACES OF INTEREST

❶ The Royal Hospital
Best known as the home of the Chelsea Pensioners, renowned for their distinctive scarlet uniforms, and as the venue for the annual Royal Horticultural Society's Chelsea Flower Show, the Royal Hospital was established by King Charles II in 1682 to take care of veterans. Originally, only men were offered places at the hospital, but since 2002, women have also been included.

❷ National Army Museum
Relating the history of the British Army, the museum was established by royal charter in 1960. Prior to its temporary closure in 2014, the permanent exhibitions were arranged chronologically, but after it reopens in 2016, these will be changed to thematic displays. It also includes an art gallery containing works by Reynolds, Gainsborough and Whistler among others.

❸ Chelsea Physic Garden
Founded in 1673 to train apprentice apothecaries, this delightful garden focuses on plants of medicinal interest and contains some fascinating features, including the oldest rock garden in England on public view, which is partly made from stones taken from the Tower of London, and pieces of Icelandic lava brought back by Sir Joseph Banks.

❹ Royal Albert Hall
From demonstrations of electric light to tennis tournaments and major theatrical performances, the Albert Hall has an unparalleled history when it comes to the figures that have performed within its walls. Well known for the annual series of Proms concerts, the hall has lived up to the aspiration of its namesake, Prince Albert, in offering a venue that would 'promote understanding and appreciation of the arts and sciences'.

❺ Imperial College
Dedicated to the study of science, engineering, medicine and business, this educational

establishment has become one of the foremost centres of research in the world. Imperial College's South Kensington campus is based around the former Imperial Institute, which was created in 1887 to celebrate Queen Victoria's Golden Jubilee. The central tower still survives.

6 The Museums of Albertopolis
Take your pick of the cream of London's museums that lie at the heart of Albertopolis: the Natural History Museum offers exhibitions based on the 80 million items that form its five main collections – with everything from dinosaur skeletons to Charles Darwin's specimens; the Science Museum's exhibits range from Robert Stephenson's famous *Rocket* to the first typewriter and a replica of Crick and Watson's model of DNA. The youngest of the museums is the Victoria & Albert, which covers some 5,000 years of art, with its superlative collections. It also houses the National Art Library.

7 Michelin Building
Designed by François Espinasse as the London headquarters of the Michelin Company, this beautiful art deco-style building retains its links to the tyre manufacturer thanks to a series of beautiful stained-glass windows featuring scenes from its adverts, and a number of ceramic tiles that feature sports cars. The building now contains a restaurant (called Bibendum after the Michelin Man), an oyster bar and the Conran Shop.

8 Sloane Square
Perpetually associated with Sloane Rangers, this Knightsbridge square is home to the Royal Court Theatre, which is renowned for premiering new works by playwrights. Designed by the architects Henry Holland Snr and Jr in 1771, the square is adorned by Gilbert Ledward's 1953 Venus Fountain.

TO THE HEIGHTS OF HAMPSTEAD HEATH

Work your way from the entertainments of Islington via the home of Arsenal Football Club and a wildlife haven to the pleasant green pastures of parks and on to the genteel sophistication of one of London's oldest villages.

DISTANCE 15km (9⅓ miles)
PROFILE Lots of climbing, some of it very steep
PICK UP DOCKING STATION Cloudesley Road, Angel
DROP OFF DOCKING STATION Castlehaven Road, Camden Town

- Ride north up Cloudesley Road away from Tolpuddle Street.
- At the modal filter turn left and right to continue north on Thornhill Road.
- At the T-junction, turn right on Offord Road and immediately left onto Westbourne Road.
- At the T-junction, turn right onto MacKenzie Road.
- At the traffic lights go straight ahead on Palmer Place.
- At the traffic lights go straight ahead on Drayton Park.
- Take the first left onto Benwell Road.
- Continue into Hornsey Road.
- At the Emirates Stadium, turn right up the ramp onto the stadium podium.
- Keep right to cross the footbridge, then turn left onto Drayton Park.
- Follow the road bending right past Arsenal Underground Station into Gillespie Road.
- Turn left and immediately right across Blackstock Road onto Mountgrove Road.
- Turn left onto Finsbury Park Road; cross Brownswood Road with care to continue on Finsbury Park Road.

- Cross the Seven Sisters Road into Finsbury Park.
- Turn left on the park road to climb past the tennis courts.
- As you pass the tennis courts near the top of the hill, turn left to exit the park on the long footbridge over the railway.
- At the other end of the bridge, turn right onto the Parkland Walk.
- Continue up the Parkland Walk railway path to the exit – uphill to the right – onto Holmesdale Road.
- Turn right up Holmesdale Road and then right at the T-junction on Archway Road.
- Turn left at the traffic lights onto Jacksons Lane.
- At the top of Jacksons Lane, turn left into Southwood Lane and at the mini-roundabout turn right onto Highgate High Street.
- Go straight on at the next mini-roundabout and at the following one turn left down Hampstead Lane, then take the first left onto The Grove.
- Turn right onto the gated road of Fitzroy Park.
- Descend Fitzroy Park with care; watch out for speed-humps and pedestrians.
- At the T-junction at the bottom of Fitzroy Park, turn right onto Millfield Lane.
- Turn right onto the footpath across the dam with the Men's Swimming Pond on your right. At the complex of paths at the end of the dam go straight ahead up the hill.
- On top of the hill, bear left on the wooded path, then keep right to emerge on the dam below the Mixed Swimming Pond.
- Bear left, then fork right across the car-parks to exit the Heath and cross East Heath Road into Downshire Hill.
- Climb to the T-junction with Rosslyn Hill and turn left down through Belsize Park and Chalk Farm.
- Where all traffic on Chalk Farm Road is forced left into Castlehaven Road, you will find the docking station on your right.

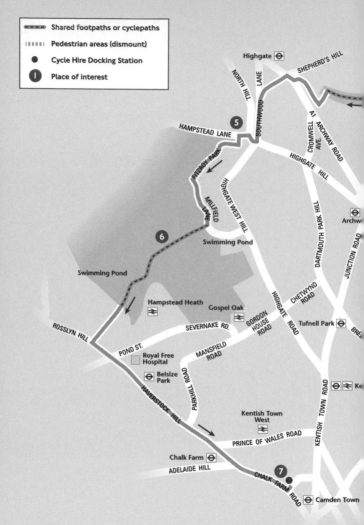

TO THE HEIGHTS OF
HAMPSTEAD HEATH

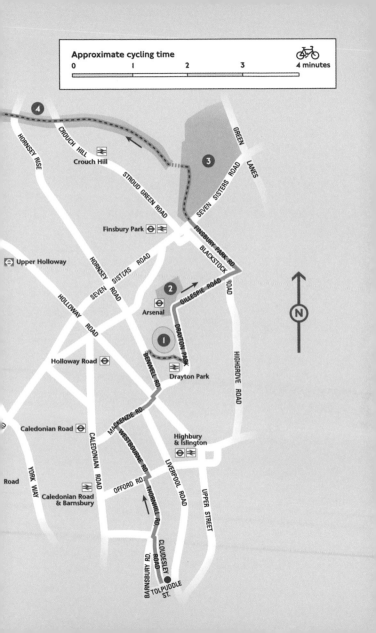

Approximate cycling time

0   1   2   3   4 minutes

HORNSEY RISE

CROUCH HILL

Crouch Hill

STROUD GREEN ROAD

GREEN LANES

SEVEN SISTERS ROAD

3

Finsbury Park

FINSBURY PARK RD.

Upper Holloway

HORNSEY ROAD

SEVEN SISTERS ROAD

BLACKSTOCK ROAD

2

Arsenal

GILLESPIE ROAD

HOLLOWAY ROAD

1

DRAYTON PARK

HIGHGROVE ROAD

Holloway Road

BENWELL RD.

Drayton Park

MACKENZIE RD.

Caledonian Road

CALEDONIAN ROAD

WESTBOURNE RD.

Highbury & Islington

York Way

YORK WAY

Caledonian Road & Barnsbury

OFFORD RD.

THORNHILL RD.

LIVERPOOL ROAD

UPPER STREET

Road

BARNSBURY RD.

CLOUDESLEY ROAD

TOLPUDDLE ST.

N

PLACES OF INTEREST

❶ Arsenal FC Stadium

The Gunners' home is the third largest football stadium in England and has a capacity of 60,272. It has hosted a number of international friendlies as well as major music concerts. Visitors can discover the history of the club at the nearby Arsenal Museum.

❷ Gillespie Park

This 2.8-ha (7-acre) nature reserve is home to a wealth of wildlife, including 244 species of plants, 94 species of birds and 24 types of butterflies. The site includes ponds, woodland and meadow areas and the Ecology Centre is open to visitors, offering advice on wildlife gardening and sustainable gardening. It is open daily, except when there are matches at the Emirates Stadium.

❸ Finsbury Park

Once part of Hornsey Wood, and officially opened in 1869, Finsbury Park was one of the first Victorian parks. During the Second World War, it was used to gather armaments for D-Day. These days,

the 46ha (113 acres) site hosts music festivals and concerts and has a wealth of facilities for sports enthusiasts, including an American football field.

❹ Parkland Walk

The walk follows the path of the old London & North Eastern Railway line that ran between Finsbury Park and Alexandra Palace. When the last sections of the track were lifted in 1970, the area was re-opened as a linear park. At 7.2km (4½ miles) long, it is London's longest nature reserve, and is home to more than 200 species of wild flower, as well as hedgehogs, butterflies, foxes, birds and even muntjac deer. Look out for the Marilyn Collins sculpture near the former Crouch End station.

❺ Highgate Village

Despite its association with the notorious highwayman Dick Turpin, Highgate is one of the most expensive London suburbs. It retains much of its original charm and contains many small boutiques, restaurants and pubs. Visit Highgate Cemetery to see the resting places of some notable figures, including Karl Marx, or the arts venue at Jacksons Lane.

❻ Hampstead Heath

One of the highest points in London, covering 320ha (791 acres), Hampstead Heath offers many recreational opportunities, such as an athletics track, ponds for swimming and children's play areas. The three ponds that lie along its eastern edge were originally reservoirs for drinking water from the River Fleet. The heath was mentioned in records as far back as AD986 and lies next to Kenwood House, where open-air concerts are held during the summer months, and part of whose grounds has been designated a Site of Special Scientific Interest.

❼ Camden Market

Comprising a number of different areas, the markets in Camden are so popular that Camden Town Tube station has restricted access to platforms on Sunday afternoons. Camden Lock Market, next to the Regent's Canal, focuses on crafts. The Stables Market, the largest of the markets in the Camden area, is housed in what was originally a Victorian horse hospital. Outlets sell a variety of handcrafted goods from clothes to jewellery and furniture, as well as antiques.

VICTORIA,
ELIZABETH & LEA

Relax in the surroundings of Victoria Park before heading
to the attractions of the Queen Elizabeth II Olympic Park
and then, if you can tear yourself away, carry on across the
Lea Valley to the home of London's Sunday League football
on Hackney Marshes.

DISTANCE 7km (4⅓ miles) round trip; easily shortened to 5km
(3 miles) by cutting off the northern loop
PROFILE Some gentle climbing and a few bridge ramps
PICK UP DOCKING STATION Cadogan Close, Victoria Park
DROP OFF DOCKING STATION As above

- From the docking station, go north (left) on Cadogan Terrace and
  shortly right down Cadogan Close to go up and over the ramped
  footbridge.
- At the foot of the bridge, go across Rothbury Road and into Wallis Road.
- Turn left at the T-junction to go under the railway bridge at Hackney
  Wick Station.
- At the crossroads turn right to stay on Wallis Road.
- At the end of Wallis Road use the lift to go up to the footbridge,
  cross the River Lea Navigation and enter the Queen Elizabeth II
  Olympic Park.
- With the Copper Box Arena on your right, climb to pass the giant
  'N' of 'Run'.
- Cross Waterden Road with care on the zebra crossing and continue
  along the very broad avenue that's actually a bridge over a channel
  of the River Lea.
- Keep left as the avenue rises and bear left to pass in front of the
  Timber Lodge Café.

- Pass the west end of the VeloPark, with it on your right, and cross the bridge over the M11 Link Road.
- Bear left to cross the bridge over Eastway. Roll down the ramp and turn left and immediately right, to carry straight on along the edge of the field with the river behind the hedge on your left.
- Turn left to cross the footbridge.
- (If you want to cut the route to 5km/3 miles, go ahead across the flat grass of Hackney Marshes on the unsurfaced path, go through the band of trees to find the River Lea Navigation and turn left.)
- Turn right on the River Road.
- Follow the path as it bends to the left and out into the open.
- Aim for the old brick changing rooms and pass with them on your left and Cow Bridge – with its new companion footbridge – on your right.
- Run south, parallel to the Navigation. The path on the edge of the marshes is easier than the towpath beside the water, where you may have to watch out for boat residents.
- (The shortcut on the unsurfaced path rejoins the route from the left.)
- Rejoin the towpath under the bridge carrying Homerton Road.
- Continue south on the towpath. Immediately before the footbridge with a lift on the other end, turn left to climb the hairpin ramp up to bridge level.
- Turn right cross the bridge and descend in the lift.
- Retrace your route along Wallis Road to the ramped footbridge.
- Cross the bridge to Cadogan Close, and turn left back to the docking station.

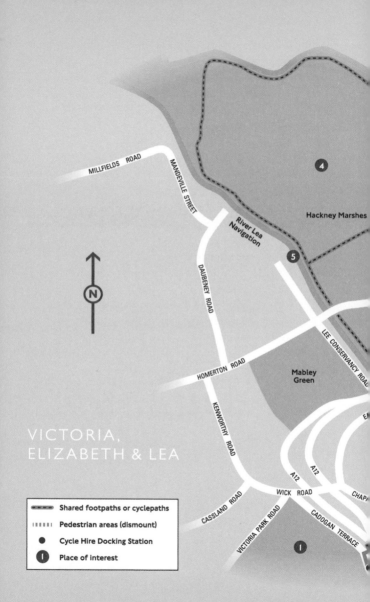

VICTORIA,
ELIZABETH & LEA

MILLFIELDS ROAD

MANDEVILLE STREET

River Lea
Navigation

DAUBENEY ROAD

HOMERTON ROAD

KENWORTHY ROAD

Hackney Marshes

4

5

LEE CONSERVANCY ROAD

Mabley
Green

A12

WICK ROAD

CASSLAND ROAD

VICTORIA PARK ROAD

CADOGAN TERRACE

CHAP

1

Shared footpaths or cyclepaths

Pedestrian areas (dismount)

● Cycle Hire Docking Station

1 Place of interest

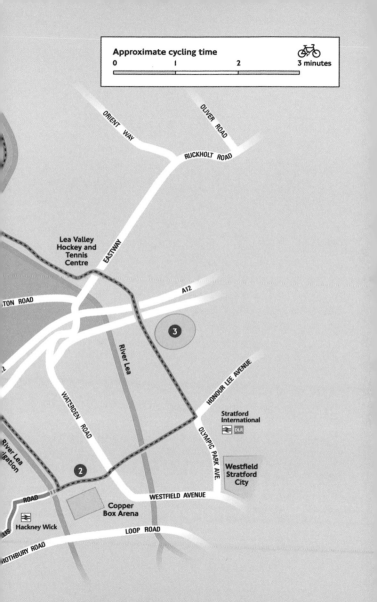

PLACES OF INTEREST

❶ Victoria Park
(See page 47.)

❷ The Queen Elizabeth II Olympic Park
(See page 87.)

❸ Lea Valley VeloPark
Of all the 2012 Olympic venues, the VeloPark saw the most victories by Team GB, with 24 medals (including 12 gold) won by the Olympic and Paralympic teams. The VeloPark has a capacity of 6,000, as does the BMX Track. There is also a 1.6-km (1-mile) road course and a mountain bike track. Covering approximately 10 ha (24½ acres), the park hosted its first international competition in 2011, the UCI BMX Supercross World Cup. Eco-friendly, the VeloPark won a number of design awards, such as the RIBA Stirling Prize for Architecture in 2011 and the 2012 Architecture Award from the Design Museum.

❹ Hackney Marshes
The marshes that existed in this area were formed by the flooding of the old River Lea and were continually drained from medieval times. Used as a dumping ground in the Second World War for the rubble caused by bombing, the marshes are best known as a venue for Sunday League football. The award-winning Hackney Marshes Centre overlooks the 138ha (340 acres) of parkland and can be used for conferences, weddings and other events.

❺ Lea Navigation
Running from the Hertford Castle Weir to Bow Creek, this waterway consists of part of the River Lea which was turned into a canal by an Act of Parliament in 1767. The River Lea had long been used to bring grain into London from Hertfordshire, and locals used it for a multitude of needs, including a water supply and for milling, as well as for pleasure. Izaak Walton wrote *The Compleat Angler* using his experiences of fishing the river.

BARNES, BIRDS, BOATS & BEACHES

Green pastures beckon as this route moves along the old streets of Barnes Village to the watery delights of an old reservoir and stretches of the Thames Path. Take time out to sit and watch nature at its best amidst the hustle and bustle of city life.

DISTANCE 6km (3¾ miles) round trip
PROFILE Flat and easy
PICK UP DOCKING STATION Bridge Avenue, Hammersmith
DROP OFF DOCKING STATION as above

- Go south on Bridge Avenue, away from King's Street, towards Great West Road.
- Use the light-controlled crossings to go under the flyover into Bridge View.
- At the end of Bridge View, turn left to reach Hammersmith Bridge Road.
- Turn right on Hammersmith Bridge Road and ride over the bridge.
- Continue on Castelnau.
- Turn right into Church Road at the light-controlled junction with the Extreme Design showroom on the corner.
- After the pond in Barnes Village, bear right into Barnes High Street.
- Take the second exit at the roundabout and cycle east along the river.
- As the road leaves the river front, divert left on the tree-lined river path.
- Follow the 'Leg of Mutton Reservoir' signposts, through the gate; this path will lead you back to the main river path.
- Continue downstream to Hammersmith Bridge.
- Immediately before the bridge, turn right up to the join the road and left to cross Hammersmith Bridge.
- Turn left to retrace your route to the docking station.

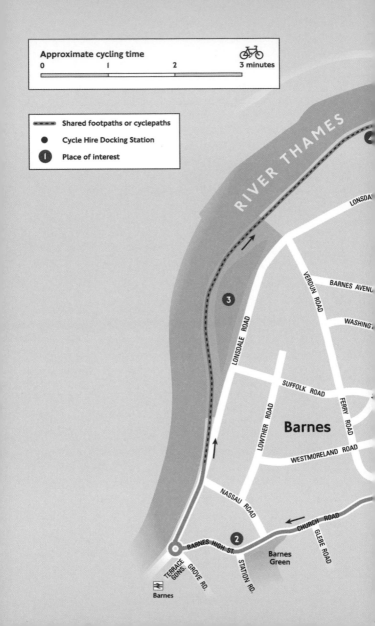

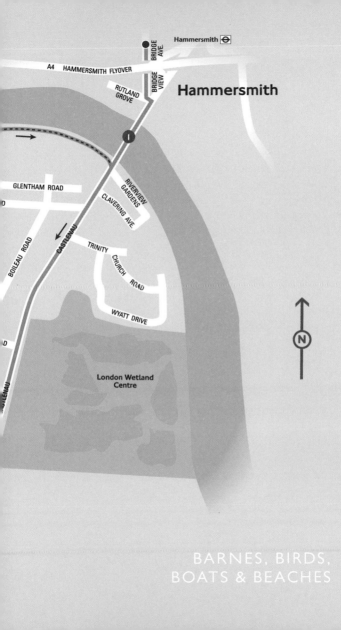

Hammersmith ●

A4 HAMMERSMITH FLYOVER

BRIDGE AVE.

BRIDGE VIEW

RUTLAND GROVE

Hammersmith

GLENTHAM ROAD

RIVERVIEW GARDENS

CLAVERING AVE.

BOILEAU ROAD

CASTLENAU

TRINITY

CHURCH ROAD

WYATT DRIVE

N

London Wetland
Centre

CASTLENAU

BARNES, BIRDS,
BOATS & BEACHES

PLACES OF INTEREST

❶ Hammersmith Bridge
(See page 113.)

❷ Barnes Village
This popular area of south-west London has maintained a 'village' atmosphere and many of the original 18th- and 19th-century houses in the streets close to Barnes Pond add to its charm. First mentioned in the Domesday Book as 'Berne', the village has some excellent shops and has been a popular place of residence for many well-known figures, including the writers Henry Fielding and Dodie Smith, and a number of actors, composers and musicians. It was sadly the site of the car accident that killed the singer Marc Bolan in 1977; a commemorative statue was unveiled in 1997 to commemorate the 20th anniversary of his death.

❸ Leg of Mutton Reservoir
Saved from development by local residents, this former reservoir is now home to a variety of water birds. The reservoir was built in 1838 and was in use until 1960.

At this site of 8ha (20 acres), it is possible to see swans, herons and grebe as well as duck and teal.

❹ The Thames Path
This was set up as a National Trail in 1996, and it is now possible to walk the length of the Thames from its source in Gloucestershire to the Thames Barrier. At 296km (184 miles) long, the path offers stretches that can be cycled along as well. Most of the path is based on the original Thames towpath. However, partly due to development, though mainly because the original users of the towpath would cross the river at various points, there are some places where the path actually diverges from the river. Walking any stretch makes a pleasant interlude and offers great views of both sides of the Thames.

BY WATER TO CHISWICK HOUSE

Dawdle along this western stretch of the Thames from Hammersmith to Chiswick and take in some of the quaint pubs and historical curiosities along the way. Finish your trip by visiting the neo-Palladian magnificence of Chiswick House with its refreshing grounds.

DISTANCE 5km (3 miles) round trip

PROFILE Flat and easy

PICK UP DOCKING STATION Bridge Avenue, Hammersmith

DROP OFF DOCKING STATION As above

- Go south on Bridge Avenue towards Great West Road. Use the light-controlled crossings to go under the flyover into Bridge View.
- At the end of Bridge View, go straight on alongside Hammersmith Bridge, down to the river and turn right onto the river path.
- Pass Furnivall Gardens on your right, and continue down the alleyway with care – walking may be necessary – with the Dove Pub on your left.
- Continue on the river path, pass Kelmscott House, home of the William Morris Society, on your right.
- At The Old Ship pub, go around the playground and exit into Chiswick Mall to run parallel to the Thames, with Hammersmith Terrace between you and the water.
- At St Nicholas' Church, turn right so the church is on your left.
- Dismount and walk through the churchyard and straight on along an alleyway called Powell's Walk.
- At the end of the alley, turn left onto Burlington Lane. The footpaths are dual-use, so you may ride on them if you prefer.
- The entrance to Chiswick House and grounds is on the right.
- Retrace the route to return to Hammersmith.

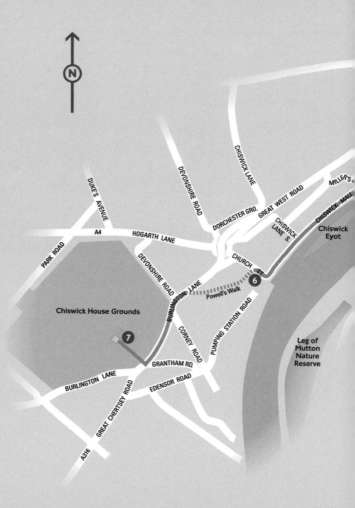

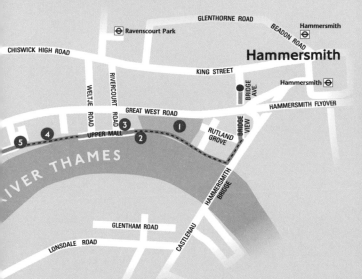

GLENTHORNE ROAD

BEADON ROAD

Hammersmith ⊖

CHISWICK HIGH ROAD

Ravenscourt Park ⊖

Hammersmith

KING STREET

Hammersmith ⊖

WELTJE ROAD

RIVERCOURT ROAD

GREAT WEST ROAD

BRIDGE AVE.

HAMMERSMITH FLYOVER

⑤ ④ ③ ① UPPER MALL ② RUTLAND GROVE

BRIDGE VIEW

RIVER THAMES

HAMMERSMITH BRIDGE

GLENTHAM ROAD

LONSDALE ROAD

CASTLENAU

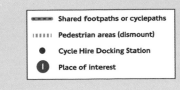

▬▬▬ Shared footpaths or cyclepaths

⋮⋮⋮⋮ Pedestrian areas (dismount)

● Cycle Hire Docking Station

❶ Place of interest

Approximate cycling time

0   1   2   3 minutes

PLACES OF INTEREST

❶ Furnivall Gardens
Named after Dr Frederick Furnivall, the gardens stand on what was the mouth of Hammersmith Creek, which had a thriving fishing business and where malt houses were built to service the local Hammersmith Brewery.

❷ The Dove
This Grade II-listed pub has what is probably the smallest bar in the world. Famous visitors include Ernest Hemingway and Graham Greene. It is said that Scottish poet James Thomson composed the words of 'Rule, Britannia' here.

❸ William Morris Society & Museum
The society and museum are based in what was Morris' last home. Containing artefacts belonging to the designer, poet and novelist, there is also an archive of books and samples of his wallpaper and textile designs.

❹ The Old Ship
Providing ale to locals since 1722, the Old Ship with its maritime artefacts is an excellent place to watch the watery world of the Thames drift by.

❺ The Black Lion
This Grade II-listed, 18th-century hostelry lies at the end of Black Lion Lane, once famous for the 'Hammersmith Ghost'.

❻ St Nicholas' Church and William Hogarth's Tomb
The site lies near a former ferry river crossing, and it is believed that a pagan shrine once existed here. A number of notable historical figures are buried in the churchyard, including William Hogarth, J.M. Whistler and Henry Joy, who sounded the trumpet at the Charge of the Light Brigade.

❼ Chiswick House
Built by the 3rd Earl of Burlington with interiors designed by William Kent, the house is one of the best examples of neo-Palladian design in Britain. The grounds are beautiful and the conservatory houses probably the oldest collection of camellias under glass.

DEER WATCHING IN RICHMOND PARK

Go out of bounds (the docking zone, that is) for a trip to Richmond Park. Enjoy the beauty of Barnes Common before heading to London's largest royal park with its ponds and gardens and take in a little deer-spotting.

DISTANCE Hammersmith to Richmond Park, 5km (3 miles)
One lap of Richmond Park, 11km (6¾ miles)
Richmond Park to Putney, 4km (2½ miles)
Total 20km (12½ miles)
PROFILE Varied with some steep descents and ascents
PICK UP DOCKING STATION Bridge Avenue, Hammersmith
DROP OFF DOCKING STATION Disraeli Road, Putney or Putney Rail Station, Putney

- Go south on Bridge Avenue, away from King's Street, towards Great West Road.
- Use the light-controlled crossings to go under the flyover into Bridge View.
- At the end of Bridge View, turn left to reach Hammersmith Bridge Road.
- Turn right on Hammersmith Bridge Road and ride over the bridge.
- Continue on Castelnau.
- At the traffic-light junction, continue straight on into Rocks Lane.
- On Barnes Common, turn right onto Mill Hill Road.
- (If you want to save time, continue on Rocks Lane to the Upper Richmond Road, turn right and then first left into Priory Lane.)
- At the mini-roundabout take the first exit onto Station Road.
- Turn right into Vine Road and go over two railway crossings.
- At the Upper Richmond Road, go straight on into Priory Lane.

- Enter Richmond Park at Roehampton Gate.
- At the mini-roundabout take the first exit – into Priory Lane – to follow the road round the perimeter of the park.
- (There is also a dirt-track path running between the road and the edge of the Park, shared with pedestrians and with more ascents and descents.)
- At the mini-roundabout take the second exit into Broomfield Hill.
- At the mini-roundabout take the second exit into Queens Road.
- At the mini-roundabout take the second exit into Sawyers Hill.
- At the mini-roundabout take the first exit to leave the park through Roehampton Gate and run down Priory Lane to the Upper Richmond Road.
- Turn right onto the Upper Richmond Road, and at the next junction fork left into Queens Ride.
- (If you want to save time, stay on the Upper Richmond Road all the way to the docking station at Putney Rail Station.)
- On Queens Ride take the second exit at the mini-roundabout – to go straight on – and immediately right into St Mary's Grove.
- At the end of St Mary's Grove, go through the modal filter at the narrow gap and straight on into Dryburgh Road.
- Continue on Dryburgh Road, and straight on into Clarendon Drive.
- At the T-junction, turn right through the modal filter.
- Turn left into one-way Chelverton Road.
- (Travelling from Putney to Richmond Park you can use Norroy Road, parallel, one block south.)
- At the T-junction, turn right onto Putney High Street.
- Disraeli Road is the first turning on the left.

PLACES OF INTEREST

❶ Barnes Common

Owned by the Dean and
Chapter of St Paul's Cathedral,
but administered by the Borough
of Richmond upon Thames, this
51-ha (127-acre) common is one
of the largest in Greater London.
A designated nature reserve, the
common is home to a variety
of birds and animals that nest
in the woods and scrubland.
Try the designated nature trail
or look for the Burnet rose (the
symbol of the Friends of Barnes
Common) that grows in profusion.
Once used by drovers as a resting
point on their way to the London
markets, the common is also
used for sports and includes
a football pitch.

❷ Richmond Park

This is the largest of London's
eight Royal Parks and a National
Nature Reserve. On a clear
day, from its highest point,
King Henry's Mound, you can
see across the city to St Paul's
Cathedral. Charles I, who moved
the court to Richmond Palace to
avoid the plague in 1625, turned

the area from a mixture of small
farms and pastureland into a park
filled with red and fallow deer that
continue to graze the park today.
Areas have been given over to
sports pitches and there is also
a golf course. The park contains
various lodges, which include
White Lodge, the home of the
Royal Ballet School.

❸ Pembroke Lodge Café

The former home of Lord John
Russell, one of Queen Victoria's
prime ministers, the lodge was
home to the GCHQ's Phantom
Squad during the Second World
War, which included the actor
David Niven. Now housing
the Hearsum Collection, which
is devoted to the heritage of
Richmond Park, the lodge has
excellent tea rooms.

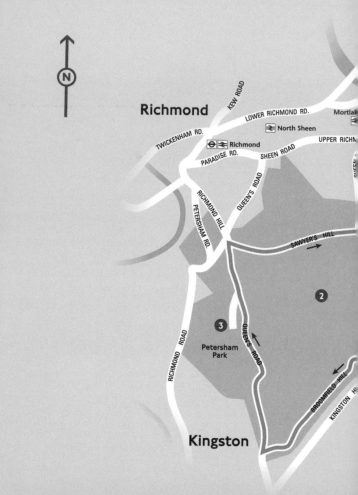

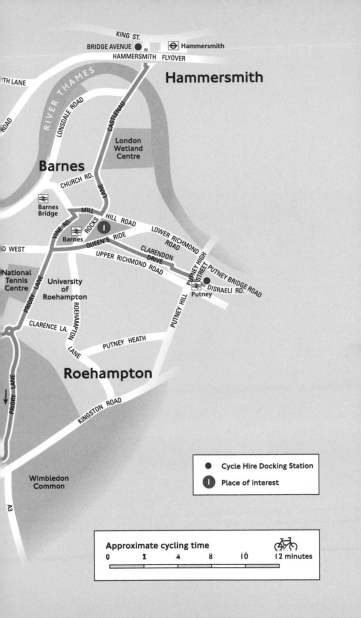

1 3 5 7 9 10 8 6 4 2

First published in 2015 by Ebury Press, an imprint of Ebury Publishing

Ebury Press is part of the Penguin Random House group of companies whose addresses can be found at global.penguinrandomhouse.com

Penguin
Random House
UK

A CIP catalogue record for this book is available from the British Library

ORIGINAL CONCEPT Victoria Marshallsay
PROJECT EDITOR Victoria Marshallsay
DESIGN Jim Smith
MAPS Transport for London
WRITERS Patrick Field (www.londonschoolofcycling.co.uk), Vanessa Daubney and Bianca Sainty (www.sainty.net)

Printed and bound in China by Toppan Leefung Printing LTD

ISBN 9780091960230

Penguin Random House is committed to a sustainable future for our business, our readers and our planet. This book is made from Forest Stewardship Council® certified paper.